# THE PROBLEM OF
# JOHN FORD

# THE PROBLEM OF
# JOHN FORD

### H. J. OLIVER

M.A. (SYD.)

*Senior Lecturer in English*
*University of Sydney*

## MELBOURNE UNIVERSITY PRESS

*First published 1955*

*Printed and bound in Australia by*
*Melbourne University Press, Carlton, N.3, Victoria*

*Registered in Australia for transmission*
*by post as a book*

*London and New York: Cambridge University Press*

# PREFACE

THE STUDY which follows, although it does, I believe, contribute to our actual knowledge of the work of Ford, is intended to be primarily a critical assessment. Accordingly, I do not think there is any serious overlapping with Miss M. Joan Sargeaunt's *John Ford*, to which I am frequently indebted for biographical and bibliographical information.

To my mind incomparably the finest critical study of Ford's plays is the chapter in Professor Una Ellis-Fermor's *Jacobean Drama*. When I began to study and expound to students Ford's movement towards and perhaps beyond 'the frontiers of drama' (a movement which regrettably makes necessary a chronological treatment of his work) I had not read that book, and I differ from it in, for example, my comparison of '*Tis Pitty* and *The Broken Heart*, but I am not concerned to limit, still less to deny, general indebtedness to it.

My quotations from Ford's unaided plays are from the best edition, Bang's *Materialien zur Kunde des älteren Englischen Dramas*, vols. xiii, xxiii and (as continued by Henry De Vocht) new series vol. i. Collaborate plays and non-dramatic works are quoted from the first edition or from manuscript, unless otherwise noted. All quotations are as exact as I can make them, except that I have disregarded the long S. At risk of being thought pedantic, but in the desirable interests of accuracy and uniformity, I spell the titles of Ford's plays as they appear on the original title-pages (except that *Loves Sacrifice* actually appeared as *Loues*).

For generous grants which made possible the purchase of photostats and otherwise helped in the completion and publication of the book, I gladly express my thanks to the Research Committee of the University of Sydney. To my colleagues Mr R. G. Howarth and Professor W. Milgate, for advice and help whenever it was sought, I am deeply indebted; and Professor I. R. Maxwell and Dr. Harold Jenkins read the typescript and saved me from more than one error. Nor would I willingly pass over the help received from private and seminar discussions of the plays with Honours students, whose ideas I must sometimes have adopted or adapted. Particularly I would mention Mrs J. Alexander, who made the plays her special study for some time, and Mr A. A. Banning.

Other invaluable assistance, at all stages of the book's preparation, was given by my wife.

H. J. OLIVER

University of Sydney, 1953

# CONTENTS

# I

## THE DRAMATIST IN HIS AGE

To READ the plays of John Ford in isolation is to examine a conclusion without the beginning. His works come at the very end of a long tradition of which he apparently had excellent knowledge; and it would seem—although of this there is, of course, no proof—that he expected similar knowledge in at least the better part of his audience, the part to which he so often, in his prologues, appealed.

Of the many great writers who had contributed to the development of English drama, most had died before Ford wrote his first unaided play. But there was no break in the tradition; and that it suggests this continuity is the one great advantage of the term 'Elizabethan' as applied to the whole period from Lyly to the closing of the theatres. Attempts to divide these years into periods corresponding to the reigning sovereigns, even as modified in Dr G. B. Harrison's division[1] into the Elizabethan period (with Marlowe as the dominant writer), the Jacobean (Shakespeare, Chapman and Ben Jonson) and the Caroline (Beaumont and Fletcher), are accordingly bound to fail; the facts of collaboration are sufficient to show how misleading are the groupings. Literary types grow, are transformed and are abandoned, as was the revenge tragedy; but the changes become noticeable so gradually that they are hard to define.

It is nevertheless worth while to try to establish some of the differences between the period of Ford and the period of Shakespeare. Perhaps the most important is a change of attitude towards drama itself. Had Ben Jonson published his 'Works' in the fourth decade of the century instead of the second, it is certain that he would not have met with the same ridicule; the average playwright's attitude to his work had become more responsible. It would not be true to say that by 1630 plays were for the first time in English literary history regarded primarily as literature; the statement would be doubly misleading if it seemed to imply that plays were now written for reader rather

---

[1] *Plays by Webster and Ford* (Everyman's Library, London, 1933), pp. vii–viii.

than audience or that writers like Ford were undramatic; but there was certainly among the playwrights of Ford's period a stronger sense of the lasting value of plays as literature. The first fine careless rapture of the Elizabethans had passed and with it some of the seemingly irresponsible writing of plays meant only for a moment's entertainment (although one can easily exagger- ate that irresponsibility). Symptomatic is the decrease in casual collaboration—the collaboration of Beaumont and Fletcher was so far from casual that it could be cited in support of the general- ization. In short, the Caroline playwright was coming nearer and nearer to the modern ideas of what a *writer* should be.

With this changed attitude to authorship went a different approach to subject matter. The consequent change of emphasis has been analysed by Professor F. P. Wilson in his *Elizabethan and Jacobean*[2]; and the key sentence, for present purposes, is this: 'What distinguishes the Jacobean age from the Elizabethan is its more exact, more searching, more detailed inquiry into moral and political questions and its interest in the analysis of the mysteries and perturbations of the human mind'. Inquiry, analysis—these interest the Jacobean writers, these rather than incident.

But—and this is the essential paradox of a dramatist like Ford—the playwright's interest in analysis rather than incident did not mean that he abandoned incident. On the contrary, he retained many of the stock situations of previous drama but used them casually, taking them—and the audience's know- ledge of them—for granted, so that, as Professor Ellis-Fermor has pointed out,[3] a kind of dramatic shorthand develops and a situation is expected to bring with it all the concomitant emotion and even incident that went with it in its original use. These situations, however, are often simply irrelevant in view of the dramatist's new interests; Ford for one would have done better to avoid them.

He did not avoid them, and in refusing to abandon them no doubt had in mind that less intelligent section of the audience that he might, in certain moods, have wished to forget. As a literary tradition continues too long, subjects become worn out

[2] Oxford, 1945, p. 20.
[3] *The Jacobean Drama* (London, rev. 1947), *passim*.

and are better discarded; the alternative is to try to strengthen them so that they still make an impact on the now deadened sensibility of one's audience. The methods by which the Elizabethan playwright sought to affect his audience were certainly not weak in the first place; as a result, a still stronger stimulus was needed by 1630 if that audience was to be stimulated at all—and some modern literary trends would provide the perfect parallel. That is why the Caroline dramatist turned more and more for his subject matter to the daring, the immoral, the unnatural; that is partly why Ford, among others, sought subjects like incest and adultery and was content to have Giovanni appear with Annabella's bleeding heart on his dagger.

The penalty is one that is always paid by the writer who comes at the end of a long tradition from which he is not willing or able to break away. It is perhaps not quite so serious a penalty for a dramatist as for a poet; if the essence of drama is conflict, then at least such subjects are potentially dramatic: incest, or a tendency to it, does bring one into conflict with the accepted ways of life. And that such a situation is potentially dramatic is surely more important to a student of literature than Professor Sherman's judgment that 'when the conflict of incestuous desires with the established order is presented as a genuine problem, moral anarchy can go no further'.[4] Moreover the incestuous desire is likely, in the mind of a man who does not completely yield to it, to produce internal conflict or at the very least unusual shades of feeling and emotion. Unusual shades of feeling and emotion were Ford's main interest; and in dealing with them he best showed his skill.

The pity is that he should have considered himself forced to work within the Elizabethan tradition, when his strength lay in analysis and inquiry. The alternative would have been to create a new tradition, of purely psychological drama; and no doubt it would have been better for Ford, in an absolute sense, if he had attempted to write plays of an entirely new kind. He tried instead to adapt the older traditions to his special needs and, if most of the subsequent criticism of his work is to be believed, succeeded, like the man with the donkey, in pleasing nobody.

[4] 'Forde's Contribution to the Decadence of the Drama', in Bang ed., *Materialien zur Kunde des älteren Englischen Dramas*, xxiii, p. xii.

By his extension of the range of dramatic subject matter, he offends those who like to pass moral judgments on literature; by his concessions to Elizabethan tradition, he offends sophisticated literary tastes.

The result is not only that critical opinion splits over Ford as over Byron but also that the very qualities which in another writer would be considered creditable are in Ford considered worthy of blame. For example, the verdict of the American critic Mr H. W. Wells[5] that it is 'with Cavalier slipperiness as much as with tragic insight (that) he ascribes some nobility to Giovanni's character' begins with the assumption that the man with incestuous leanings must be wholly bad and ends in effect by calling a dramatist's ability to win sympathy for his characters a defect. This is surely the reduction of dramatic criticism to absurdity.

Equally beside the point would be the typical moral criticism of Ford, who naturally receives special condemnation in a study called *The Moral Tone of Jacobean and Caroline Drama* (Amsterdam, 1930). Writing of *'Tis Pitty*, the author, Dr Bastiaenen, comments:

> Whatever moral objections may be raised to other plays on the same theme, they are nowhere so numerous and so appalling as in this tragedy by Ford. Just as in the preceding drama (Beaumont and Fletcher's *A King and No King*) both the man and the woman indulge in the vicious passion, and they are brother and sister. The crime is not averted but actually committed. Whereas in *A King and No King* there was, at least, a strong endeavour to fight the powerful temptation, there is here a lamentable want of backbone and a deplorable effeminacy, especially in the conduct of the man. It is true, at the urgent request of the friar, Giovanni tries to eradicate his morbid propensity by having recourse to a week's seclusion and prayer, but we know beforehand that the result will be negative. As usual, fate is again denounced as the real culprit. Giovanni has at his disposal no end of sophistic, casuistic arguments, which he derives from anything, even from his nearness in blood to his sister. And the whole is suffused with sweet, luscious, lyrical poetry, often of such charming beauty that we heartily regret that it should have been uttered in such an objectionable cause. Whereas transgressors of this sort, as is evident from the plays already discussed, are, in the majority of cases, morally depraved people, the two presented here are of a different type. The young man is conspicuous for both his mental and moral

[5]*Elizabethan and Jacobean Playwrights* (New York, 1939), p. 51.

good qualities . . . The young lady also, at the outset, is represented
as an amiable, well-conducted woman, but we soon realize that she
is no whit better than her brother. There is about her an atmosphere
of impurity, which manifests itself in the sickly, extravagant praise
of her brother's good outward parts, and she goes on with this
nauseous commendation, even when she stands face to face with her
husband after the detection. The only extenuating circumstance in
her favour is the baneful influence exercised upon her by the abomin-
able nurse, but the latter is more than compensated by that
admirable friar, who, if to some extent a slave to convention, is an
excellent spiritual counsellor. Here, too, the wages of sin is death,
but it may be argued against the dramatist, that the sensational
manner, in which both Annabel and Giovanni depart this life, the
latter while parading Annabel's heart on the point of his dagger,
looks very much like an 'apotheosis of crime'. So far from acting as a
stern censor of such criminal aberrations as occur in this play, Ford
looks upon them with a lenient, sympathetic eye. Passion and sin,
even when of so revolting a nature as in the present instance, are
represented as irresistible, so that it is useless to fight them. Besides,
they are surrounded by a lot of argument, which may cause the
merely objective spectator to distrust his own notions of good and
evil, and to palliate the ugliness of what is morally indefensible. This
is very objectionable, for just as it goes against the grain to see crime
and vice made subjects for laughter, it should rouse our indignation
to see pity and sympathy invoked for that which really only deserves
our scorn and contempt (pp. 102–3).

Of the implications of this for dramatic criticism there is
probably no need to say much; but it is worth while pointing
out that such false assumptions—that poetry ceases to be accept-
able when it deals with immorality, that characters who are
'weak' in real life are 'lamentable' and 'deplorable' in drama,
that a dramatist is not primarily a recorder but ought to be a
'stern censor' of the morals of his characters and even a
protector of the morals of his audience—run through a great
deal of Ford criticism (including much of the American criticism) and are not infrequently combined with that same astig-
matism which, simply because of moral dislike for the main
characters of 'Tis Pitty, allows the Friar to be seen as morally
admirable, against all the evidence of the play itself.

Saintsbury's attempt to escape from the difficulty by claiming
that Ford has 'little to do with real life'[6] will bear no more
investigation than will Charles Lamb's similar defence of

[6]*Elizabethan Literature* (London, 1887), p. 402.

Restoration comedy; like Mr T. S. Eliot's claim that *Perkin Warbeck* is Ford's greatest work,[7] it is probably most significant as showing how widespread is the critical uneasiness in dealing with Ford's plays.

When we inquire into the life and character of the man who has brought such assaults upon his head, the result is by no means what those assaults would lead us to expect. The fullest account of him has been given by Miss M. Joan Sargeaunt in her *John Ford* (Oxford, 1935); briefly the facts would seem to be these.

Ford, who came of an old Devonshire landowning family, was baptized at Ilsington, Devon, in April 1586. He perhaps matriculated at Oxford in 1601, but certainly soon chose the third great Elizabethan University, the Inns of Court. He was admitted to the Middle Temple in November 1602, and there are records of his residence there for many years—at least until 1617. There is no evidence that he ever became a barrister, but Miss Sargeaunt has argued that he would hardly have lived in the Middle Temple for so long had he not actually followed the legal profession in one of its branches. It would seem highly probable that in the law courts he learnt much that was to be of value to him in his plays; he certainly insists that there was some foundation in fact (though in this case the fact belonged to the past) for the story of *The Broken Heart*, the prologue of which states that

> What may be here thought a *fiction*, when Times youth
> Wanted some riper yeares, was knowne *A Truth*.

Professor G. C. Moore Smith suggested as long ago as 1923[8] that biographers had taken too literally the reference to Ford in lines 81-2 of Hemminge's *Elegy on Randolph's Finger*

> Deep In a dumpe Iacke forde alone was gott
> Wth folded Armes and Melancholye hatt.

The lines, he suggested, are not a description of Ford but a literary allusion to his *Lovers Melancholy*, the symptoms described being simply the traditional marks of the melancholy lover.

---

[7] *Elizabethan Essays* (London, 1934), p. 146.
[8] William Hemminge, *Elegy on Randolph's Finger*, ed. G. C. Moore Smith (Oxford, 1923), p. 24.

Ford likes to regard himself as a scholar, aiming to please the
more educated; so we have his references in his prologues and
dedications to his unwillingness to play down to uneducated
tastes, and the acknowledgement in the Prologue to *The Lovers
Melancholy* that he has not borrowed

> more then the right
> A Scholer claimes, may warrant for delight.

The commendatory verses printed with his plays are singu-
larly free from any clues to his life; references are again largely
to his literary fame and his scholarship. It might not be extreme
to argue that what is significant about the plays themselves in
this connection is how little we learn from them about the
author. My own prevailing impression of Ford is of one who
observed life quietly, and by no means without sympathy.
Havelock Ellis has already suggested[9] that Ford writes of women
as one who had loved and understood; if that is true, perhaps
the tense is as significant as the rest of the statement.

It is not always recognized that Ford was forty years of age
before he wrote his first unaided play; there is then, not surprisingly, something in the tone of them that reminds one at
times of another middle-aged observer, Samuel Richardson.

Ford seems to have come to full dramatic authorship very
gradually indeed. It has been shown that his works fall naturally
into three groups:

(1) a period of non-dramatic work from 1606 to 1620,
(2) a period of dramatic work in collaboration, from 1621 to
    1625,
(3) a period of unaided dramatic work, from 1628 to at least
    1638. (It is not known when Ford died and he might even
    have lived in retirement until the Restoration.)

A brief glance at the first group will perhaps not be out of
place. It must be confessed that Ford's non-dramatic work is
of no great literary importance, but it has at least the interest
that the non-dramatic work of a great playwright always has:
it shows whether the writer's gift was purely dramatic in nature;
and it gives some hope of finding out a little about the man
himself.

[9] *John Ford*, in the 'Mermaid' series (London, 1888), p. xvii.

## II

## THE NON-DRAMATIC WORK

A FULL LIST of the non-dramatic works known to be by Ford or ascribed to him on reasonable evidence would be:

1606  *Fames Memoriall* (a poem)

1606  *Honor Triumphant* (a prose pamphlet)

1613  *Christes Bloodie Sweat* (a poem)

1613  *The Golden Meane* (a prose pamphlet)

1615  *Sir Thomas Overburyes Ghost* (probably another pamphlet but not extant)

1620  *A Line of Life* (a prose pamphlet)

*Fames Memoriall* was published in 1606 and also survives in a manuscript version.[1] The poem is an elegy on the Earl of Devonshire and is dedicated to the Countess; Malone himself was the first to suggest that the manuscript was the presentation copy.

The suggestion was accepted by Mr Bertram Lloyd[2] and by Miss Sargeaunt; but to the best of my knowledge no actual collation of the texts has been published. The manuscript has better readings in some lines, where perhaps the quarto has a misprint or other error: for example, the manuscript's

> resolue to droppes of Sacrifice

is better than the quarto's 'two' (sig. C1$^r$);

> consist in being heavens quaint architecture

is better than the quarto's 'quaintest' (sig. E4$^r$); and

> the high deseignes to w$^{ch}$ his spirit aymd

would seem preferable to 'assigns' (sig. C1$^r$).

On the other hand, not one of these quarto readings could be called a serious error; and there are lines in the manuscript which do not make sense. The manuscript version, in a stanza describing Devonshire's fame, refers to his chivalry

---

[1] Bodleian MS. Mal. 238 (10).

[2] 'An Inedited MS. of Ford's *Fames Memoriall*', *Review of English Studies*, i (1925), 93–5.

W^ch by y^e trumpe of glorious lowdly blowne
In Courtę of greatest princes of Renowne.

One has to refer to the quarto to find that the correct reading
in the first line is not 'glorious' but 'glore was' (sig. C4^v). This
seems an odd kind of error for an author to make in writing
out his own poem as carefully as he can, although it is just
possible that he was copying mechanically from a draft. Is the
error not more probably a scribe's?

There are a few other puzzling differences between the texts.
In the main part of the poem, which is written in pentameters,
the manuscript has a line:

Deuoure them? and surfeite on the bayte.

Presumably 'deuoure' was pronounced as three syllables. The
quarto adds 'thou' after 'deuoure' (sig. E4^r), thereby treating
'deuoure' as a word of two syllables. The line is a pentameter in
either case, the alteration could have come about in several
ways, and it is difficult to say which is the 'correct' reading. But
what is the explanation of the manuscript's

Day weareth daie, houre consumeth houre

where the quarto reads

Day weareth day, howre consumes howr (sig. F2^r)?

This is from the second epitaph on Devonshire, where the poet
is writing lines of eight syllables. The quarto line is octosyllabic,
with 'howre' pronounced according to a normal poetic convention, as one syllable. The manuscript line scans only if
'houre' is pronounced at least once as a dissyllable—and the
line becomes a pentameter and to that extent odd. Presumably
the quarto reading is correct—and consistent. How then did
'consumeth' get into the manuscript? Did not Ford almost
certainly write 'consumes', sacrificing grammatical consistency
to sense and rhythmical balance? Is not 'consumeth' much
more likely to be a copyist's attempt to make the grammar consistent—not seeing that metre was also involved?[3]

Without reaching any conclusion one may enter a caveat
against too rash an assumption that the manuscript is in Ford's
own hand. It still remains true that the manuscript is more out-
spoken than the printed version, not only in the three extra

[3] It is just worth noting that in *Christes Bloodie Sweat* 'hour' is always a single
syllable, even when spelt 'hower' (p. 38).

stanzas commending the Countess for her defiance of convention
in her association with Mountjoy (Lloyd and Miss Sargeaunt
have printed transcripts of these) but also in the stanza beginning

> A beautie fairely wise; wisely discreete
> in setting nought by vulgar rumors slannder

(Quarto: in wincking mildely at the toong of rumour—sig. D4ᵛ)
from which one must, I think, conclude that the manuscript at
least represents an earlier version which was toned down before
publication.[4] This in its turn may suggest that Ford took care
with what he published—a point to be remembered when the
question of ascribing to him anonymous works is taken up.

One thing is certain: that *Fames Memoriall* has no great
literary merit. Ford confesses in the dedication that he is a mere
stranger, not known to the Countess; and therefore from the
beginning of the poem to the end he takes refuge in generalities,
with consequent exaggeration, of which

> Hee was the best, the most, most, best, of all

is unfortunately typical. Ford frequently introduces absurdity
by making the obvious explicit—for instance, in his account of
Mountjoy at school; and constantly overstates his case:

> Mountioy (the mounting ioy of heavens perfection)
> was all a man should bee in such an age.

Similarly Mountjoy's enemies are always wrong—the Irish,
particularly:

> Malice did euer blinde their senses reason.

Nor is the overstatement merely exaggeration of opinion; often
it is a matter of wording alone, as in:

> Heere hee beganne to tast the fragrant smacke
> The Catapotion of hearts rasing Loue[5]

—a sheer inability to say a plain thing plainly. A stanza
seemingly modelled on Kyd's notorious 'O eyes no eyes' would
also seem an unnecessary risk. The occasional epigram—like
the comment on Elizabeth's death before she could learn of
Mountjoy's success in Ireland

---

[4] I do not know what significance to attach to the fact (pointed out by Lloyd)
that the poet's mistress is 'flint-hearted Lucia' in the MS., 'Lycia' in the Q. She
is barely mentioned and is almost certainly a poetic fiction.

[5] I read the manuscript thus as 'rasing'; the Q. 'easing' (sig. B4ʳ) might seem to
make better sense.

The newes was happie, but for her too late

—cannot save such a poem from overwhelming monotony.

Nor has *Fames Memoriall* any great biographical significance. That Ford wrote it at all is evidence, I suppose, that he was not of those who disapproved of the marriage; and he writes of the Earl and Countess as

Linkt in the gracefull bondes of deerest lief
Vniustly tearm'd, disgracefull . . .

But he could not speak otherwise than approvingly in a poem dedicated to the Countess herself; one surely must resist what is apparently for some the strong temptation to conclude from this poem that Ford was an advocate of free love.

In the same year as *Fames Memoriall*, 1606, Ford published *Honor Triumphant: or the Peeres Challenge, by Armes defensible, at Tilt, Turney, and Barriers. In Honor of all faire Ladies, and in defence of these foure positions following. 1. Knights in Ladies service haue no free Will. 2. Beauty is the mainteiner of valour. 3. Faire Lady was neuer false. 4. Perfect louers are onely wise: Mainteined by Arguments. Also The Monarches Meeting: or The King of Denmarkes welcome into England.*

*The Monarches Meeting* consists of twenty-five four-line stanzas describing, in the most general terms, the meeting of the monarchs; fifty-two lines in which the poet 'applauds' the monarchs' meeting; and 'The applause Song for the King of Denmarkes *arriuall*' (another thirty-five lines). The language of all the verses is so hyperbolical and the straining for rhymes so obvious ('for visitation of an neighbouring mate' to rhyme with 'state'—sig. F1ᵛ) that there would be no point in dwelling on them.

Nor is there anything particularly interesting in *Honor Triumphant* itself. This type of devil's advocacy—'proving' that 'fair lady was never false'—needs, to make it worth while, wit and intellectual agility, of the kind found, say, in Donne's *Paradoxes and Problemes*. Ford has flashes of what may be humour, as when, defending the impossible, he excuses himself with 'in knowen verities many proofes are needlesse' (sig. B4ᵛ) or indulges in syllogisms (Fair lady was never false; Helen of Troy was false; therefore Helen was not fair—she was merely deemed to be so); but if parts are written with the tongue in the cheek,

others are at least half-serious and correspondingly duller. Again
the reader who inferred from this kind of advocacy any more
than a passing interest in theories of courtly love would be
making mountains out of molehills. Professor Sherman clearly
takes it all too seriously.[6]

Miss Sargeaunt has shown[7] that 'any future editor of Ford's
works should consider the inclusion in his edition of both *Christes
Bloodie Sweat* and *The Golden Meane*'. Both attributions were
made by Joseph Hunter in *Chorus Vatum*. (Hunter followed, with
the earlier of the two works, a suggestion by B. H. Bright.)

*Christes Bloodie Sweat* is a long poem, of nearly two thousand
lines, in six-line stanzas, published anonymously in 1613. It
'containes but a Summarie of the Sonne of Gods sorrowes' and
is all on the theme:

> This is a rule in text for certaine giuen,
> An eye still drie doth seldome come to heauen (p. 39).

Miss Sargeaunt's reasons for thinking it is by Ford are summarized by her thus:

The dedication, written to one of his known patrons, in the style
of his other dedications, is signed 'I.F.'. There is one striking parallel
(a passage of some length) to a passage in *'Tis Pity*. The central
idea of the poem is the one religious idea that occurs with great
frequency in Ford's plays. The word 'pearl', as always in Ford's
verse, is dissyllabic. The poem is written in the same manner and
style as *Fames Memoriall*.

I am not particularly impressed by the similarity of styles in
the dedications; and the two passages which Miss Sargeaunt
finds strikingly parallel, one in the poem and one in *'Tis Pitty'*,
could each be independently derived from the passage in Nash's
*Pierce Penniless* which she admits to be the likely source of the
lines in the poem.

But the main religious idea of the poem, that salvation is for
'the chosen and elect' and is possible only through sincere repentance, the tears washing away the sin, is certainly like the
thought of many passages in Ford's plays. Miss Sargeaunt
quotes the Friar's advice to Giovanni:

> . . . wash euery word thou vtter'st
> In teares, (and if't bee possible) of blood:
> Begge Heauen to cleanse the leprosie of Lust
> That rots thy Soule

[6]Bang, *Materialien*, vol. xxiii, Introductory Essay.    [7]*R.E.S.*, x (1934), 165-76.

and could have compared from the poem the lines (p. 36) in which Christ is said to have given His blood

> To cleanse and wash away each leprous spot
> That vse of sinne doth feed as sinne begot.

This notion of sin as a leprosy, to be washed away by repentance, is perhaps more common than has been supposed; it occurs, for example, in the ballad that may have been a source of *A Late Murther of the Sonn upon the Mother*, in lines which Miss Sargeaunt quotes merely because 'Ford may have found them suggestive'. (I shall have to return to the point in discussing *The Duke of Lerma*.) But the idea is certainly typical of Ford and its presence must be regarded as significant in a work which there are other reasons for thinking to be by him.

Of these other reasons, the dissyllabic pronunciation of 'pearl' (though again not confined to Ford) is also significant; and I am impressed by the evidence of the over-use in both *Fames Memoriall* and *Christes Bloodie Sweat* of certain forms of repetition, both within stanzas and as a link from one stanza to the next.

Accepting *Christes Bloodie Sweat*, then, as probably but not certainly by Ford, we learn from the preface 'To such as shall peruse this Booke' that the poet has come to feel (like Herbert and Cowley and Vaughan after him) that it is regrettable that 'Poetrie is so euery way made the Herauld of wantonnesse, as there is not now any thing too vncleane for lasciuious rime'.

And I, to cleere (as I might) verse, from the soyle of this vnworthinesse, haue herein (at least) proued that it may deliuer good matter, with fit harmonie of words, though I haue erred in the latter . . . I confesse, I haue, touching my perticular, beene long carried with the doubts of *folly, youth,* and *opinion,* and as long miscaried in the darknesse of vnhappinesse, both in *inuention* and *action,* This was not the path that led to a contented rest, or a respected name. In regarde whereof, I haue heere set forth the witnesse that may testifie what I desire to bee . . .

One need not believe that the author of *'Tis Pitty* was an apostle of free love, or anything like it, to feel that if this declaration is sincere (it is no doubt partly, at least, conventional), there must have been a further change of mind before the plays were penned.

More interesting than the poet's state of mind, however, is
the state of his poetry. And here there is a remarkable improvement on *Fames Memoriall*. The author has nothing novel to say;
it all resembles too closely the pious advice of the Friar which
the intellectual Giovanni found so unsatisfying because it was
of the kind that convinces only one who is already convinced.
But everything in *Christes Bloodie Sweat* is at least said clearly.
The poet is attempting also to avoid monotony; he breaks up
his narrative and exhortation with dialogue, semi-dialogue and
question and answer; and his versification shows many variations on the normal iambic pentameter: there are dozens of
reversed stresses, many lines have extra syllables (there is at
least one Alexandrine) and others gain emphasis by omission
of a syllable:

> This did the mockers of th'elect and holy,
> Whom God hath set on earth to do his will,
> Regard they could not be so curst in folly,
> As to perseuer in their mischiefe still;
> Despising Preachers, and nicke naming those,
> With malice, whom the holy ghost chose.    (p. 18)

In short, you could say of *Christes Bloodie Sweat*, as you could
not say of *Fames Memoriall*, that the author is beginning to be
interesting as a poet.

For the development of the poetic skill, however, we have to
wait for the plays. *The Golden Meane* and *A Line of Life*, the only
other two non-dramatic works of any length, are in prose.

It is in *A Line of Life* (1620)—as again Miss Sargeaunt has
pointed out—that Ford has given the clue to his authorship of
*The Golden Meane*, published anonymously in 1613. In the later
pamphlet he writes:

> In all things, no one thing can more requisitely bee observed to
> be practised, then *The Golden Meane*: The exemplification whereof,
> however heretofore attributed, I dare not so poorely vnder-value
> myselfe and labours, as not to call mine.

Once one has the clue, one sees parallels between the two
works everywhere, in theme and in treatment.

In *The Golden Meane*, '*Discoursing* The Noblenesse of perfect
Vertue in extreames', Ford argues that as judgment is to wisdom
(a matter of the mind), so moderation, the golden mean, is to

nobility (a matter of conduct). Of nobility, the real test is
adversity; and of adversity there are six outstanding forms: dis-
favour, neglect, forfeiture of estate, banishment, imprisonment
and death. But for all these there is a remedy—to adapt oneself
to the emergency, see in what ways that emergency may even
be desirable and so 'make good vse of all aduersity'. (By 'the
golden mean' Ford means something not so very different from
resignation or even stoicism; he is indeed in the important Stoic
tradition of the sixteenth and seventeenth centuries.)

His argument involves, it must be confessed, some word-
spinning, some sophistry and a great deal of platitude. If one
loses one's wealth, he reasons, there are two possibilities: either
one has earned the money by one's own efforts—in which case
one can earn again; or one has inherited it—in which case one
'doth forgo but that which hee neuer laboured for'. Or again
if one is banished, one need only reflect that many a man has
voluntarily spent years abroad as a pleasure or remember how
the banished Mowbray died gloriously when fighting the Turk
in Palestine or how the banished Richmond returned to over-
throw the wicked Richard III, and all one's troubles will presumably vanish. One is tempted, like the reader of Byron's
'Thus was Corinth lost and won', to add a Q.E.D.

Just why this kind of pamphlet should have appealed to
readers of the early seventeenth century, particularly when it is
so long (180 pages) and the prose often so involved, is a question
that may puzzle the modern reader. There cannot, obviously,
have been so many in danger of banishment that it could have
the 'practical' value of even the trite modern guides to a good
life. Yet that the work was popular and was not of interest only
to the imprisoned Northumberland to whom it is addressed, is
indicated by the appearance in 1614 of a second edition, 'Enlarged by the first Authour'.[8]

The alterations do not give any help by showing what the
author thought most important about his work. The passages

[8]There are minor differences between copies of this edition. Apparently correc-
tions were made in the usual way as the work was being printed off; so that while
the B.M. and the Bodleian copies have several misprints in common, where the
B.M. copy has 'misey' on p. 141, the Bodleian copy has 'misery'. Conversely the
bracketing on p. 26 is right in the B.M. copy, wrong in the Bodleian. It is quite
noticeable that the errors tend to occur in passages added in the second edition.

common to the two editions are all but identical, only a very
rare alteration of either spelling or punctuation being made and
an odd omission of a word being corrected. The expansions are
somewhat mechanical. The author has added four sections, each
of two or three pages, to the general argument; has added a brief
definition of a 'misery' to distinguish his six main forms of
misery or adversity from the other incidental misfortunes of
man; and then has inserted at least one set of two or three pages
into the discussion of each of those miseries. He has tried also
to strengthen the argument that leads to his conclusion that to
act wisely and to deliberate nobly is to be perfect. In thus
revising he has preserved the proportions of the original but in
spite of his new comparisons and illustrations has done little to
strengthen the argument, of which the basic weaknesses remain.

The popularity was probably, however, due to the subject
matter itself. And this is perhaps not inexplicable. It is clear that
the Elizabethans and Jacobeans had a particular interest in
moral philosophy and the elementary forms of psychology; and
when there appeared a monumental work on psychology, *The
Anatomy of Melancholy*, Ford was, one imagines, one of its most
eager readers. He was certainly one of the earliest and most
extensive borrowers from it. The other great interest of the
period, political philosophy, he does not seem to have shared;
and Machiavelli's is not a name that is found frequently in his
pages. But to these two interests, psychology and politics,
Englishmen of the Tudor period had added, naturally enough,
a third, an interest in the relationship between ruler and subject—the theme of *The Golden Meane*. Bacon's *Essaies* show that
the topic had retained its popularity; nor can it be without
significance that the enlarged edition of thirty-eight essays had
been published in 1612, just before *The Golden Meane*. Here
again, it would seem, Ford was writing on a subject which had
a special intellectual appeal to the more sophisticated readers of
his day; and the work perhaps suffers unduly in the eyes of a
modern reader because its observations have become platitu-
dinous by repetition. Ford has not the cynical turn of mind that
lends an added attractiveness to Bacon's meditations on the
same theme.

*A Line of Life. Pointing at the Immortalitie of a Vertuous Name*

(1620) is so like *The Golden Meane* both in matter and in method that it hardly requires separate mention. Ford argues, with similar illustrations from contemporary and classical history, that:

Action, perseuerance in action, and sufferance in perseuerance, are the three golden linckes y$^t$ furnishe vpp the richest chayne wherewith a *good man* cann be adorned: they are a tripertite counter-pawne, whereby we hold the possession of life, whose Charter or pole deed (as they tearme it) are youth till twenty, manhood till fforty, old age till our end. And hee whoe beginns not in the spring of his minority to budd forth fruites of virtuous hopes, or hopefull deserts, w$^{ch}$ may ripen in the sommer of confirmed manhood; rarely or never yeildes the cropp of a plentifull memory in his age, but preventє the wynter of his last houre, in the barren Autume of his worst houre, by making an even reckoning with tyme mispent, dyeing w$^{th}$out any issue to inherite his rememberance or comendation.

Heere is then a preparation made to the grounde worke & foundation, whereon y$^e$ structure and faire building of a mynde nobly furnisht must stand; w$^{ch}$ for the perpetuitie and glorie of so lasting a monument, can not altogether vnfittly be applyed to *A line of life*; ffor whosoeuer shall levell and square his whole course by this iust proportion, shall as by a lyne be ledd, not only to vnwynde himselfe from out the laborinthe & maze of this naturall & troublesome race of fraylety, but to flye vp in the midle pathe, the *via-lactea* of immortalitie in his name on earth, to the throne of life and perfection in his whole man, and to an immortality that cannot be chaunged.

Then, in the manner of the earlier work, he proceeds to subdivide, and in the rest of the treatise takes the subdivisions in turn:

Order in euery taske, is for conceipte easieste, for demonstration playnest, for immytaĉon surest. Lett vs then take into our consideration this *line of life*, and trace the waye wherein wee are to travaile, keeping our eye on the compasse whereby wee may runn to the paradise of memorable happynes: And first it is to bee obserued, that *Resolution* hath three brannches: The one concernes a manns owne perticuler person, for the carryage of himself in his proper dutie, and such a one is knowne by none other note then in beeing a man: Another concernes a mannes imployment in affaires for his country, prince, and common wealth, and such a one is knowne by the generall name of a publique man. The last concernes a mannes voluntary traffique in civill causes, without the imposition of aucthoritie, onely vrg'd on to perform the offices of a frend, or a private Statiste to seuerall endes, all tending to goodnes and virtue, and such a one is ever to be cal'd *A good man.* In euery one of those, there is a plentifull imployment, presenting it self to the liberall choice, for ennobling themselues with publicke honors, or gayning them the truest honor, *a deserued fame*; w^ch is one (if worthie,) of the best and highest rewardes of virtue.

*A Line of Life* survives also in an unpublished manuscript,[9] and a passage towards the end which is not in the printed version is practically a summary of *The Golden Meane.* Ford is saying that a man who has followed the precepts given in his pamphlet will not fail to leave a good name behind him,

howsoeuer hee live, sequestred from commerce by the iniustice of a prevayling enimye, or shutt vpp in prison by the suggestion of nimble information, or disgraced by the credulous confidence of misinformed maiestie, or dispised by the many tongu'd malice of the abused multitude, or impouerished by the oppression of an ever-begging, but a never satisfied flatterie, or defamed by the gracelesse rumour of scandale, or traduced by the juggling deceipte and snare of smoothe imposture, or (w^ch is the finishing of mischeifes and miseryes) putt to death by the importunitie of the faultie.[10]

I think this would remove any lingering doubt about the authorship of the earlier tract.

It does not seem to have occurred to anyone to compare the handwriting of this manuscript with that of the manuscript of *Fames Memoriall.* (The former is in the British Museum, the latter in Bodley.) I do not think there is any doubt that it is the same hand, although *Fames Memoriall* has been more carefully done: the writer has a peculiar way of using two forms of the letter 'r' and two of 'h' that alone would allow one to make the identification. If, then, *Fames Memoriall* is a Ford holograph, so is *A Line of Life*; the alternative is to believe that Ford in 1620 used the services of the professional scribe he had used in 1606—and that would not be by any means impossible, particularly as Ford would seem to have lived in the Middle Temple all those years.

I have shown that comparison of the printed and manuscript versions of *Fames Memoriall* throws some doubt on the identification of Ford as the writer of the manuscript; and comparison of

[9]B.M. Lans. MSS. 350.
[10]f. 181, in the original numbering. (The numbering of the pages has been twice corrected.) The two passages previously quoted I have also given, for interest, as they are in the manuscript (f. 146^v and f. 150).

the two versions of *A Line of Life* (a comparison not previously attempted, I think) raises the same doubt.

What is certain is that neither is derived directly from the other. The manuscript lacks the preface *Wise, and Therein Noble* and the corresponding section at the end called *The Corollary*; instead, it has a dedication 'To the right worthye of all honours, of all loue, Sir James Haye knight, lord Haye, viscount Doncaster, Baron of Salye, one of his Maiesties most honorable priuie Councell'. After the usual flattery (not as fulsome as the flattery of James I in the text proper) the author describes himself, in terms more suggestive of financial embarrassment, perhaps, than any he has elsewhere used, as

One so farr beneath the happynes of thriving fortunes, that hee is ambitious of beeing fortunate in no happier thrift, then y^e indeuouring to bee as I resolue to bee and am
A servant to your perfect and right accomplished virtues.

This is signed 'John de la Ford'. It is probable, then, that this manuscript, like that of *Fames Memoriall*, is a presentation copy; and behind both it and the printed version must lie at least one other manuscript, the author's original one.

The presence in the surviving manuscript of such additional passages as the one quoted above enumerating the 'miseries' of life might then be taken by those who would assume the manuscript to be a Ford holograph as afterthoughts, possibly even added as he was writing out the treatise for Viscount Doncaster. The same explanation would cover other lines, phrases and words not in the printed version, such as the additional praise of Lord Harington (f. 159), a paragraph about 'grosse and subordinate tyme pleasers' (f. 165), three phrases added to make flatterers seem even more infamous (f. 168), and the words 'stoope' and 'else' in 'whether hee stand, walke, revell, stoope, lye downe, or any way else dispose himselfe' (f. 145^v). The few trivial omissions would be understandable; and 'the miste of their misdeedes' (f. 157) and 'glory of their owne impiety' (f. 166^v) would indicate simply that the printed 'trust' and 'piety' were printer's errors.

Some of the mistakes in the manuscript would show no more than that somebody was copying carelessly, as in *Fames Memoriall*; an author making a transcript can repeat a phrase and write 'by a generall voyce by a generall smart and detryment vnto the common wealth' (f. 167ᵛ) for 'generall voyce of a generall smart . . .'; can write 'as the differed' (f. 159) for 'they', and possibly even 'by comprimittinge such passions as runn with an insurrection' (f. 176ᵛ) for 'into', and 'his owne solace is to him as an expugnable castle of strength against all the forcible assaultes of deuilishe complotts' (f. 177) for 'inexpugnable'. But it is rather harder to accept as an author's mistake 'Deceaving and deceaveable palmesters, who will vndertake by the view of the hand, to be as expert in foretelling the course of life to come to others, and they are ignorant of their owne in themselves, have found . . .' (f.147ᵛ)—instead of 'as they are ignorant' (has not the scribe misunderstood?); and I certainly question whether Ford could have written, even if copying carelessly:

Is such a mighty man intyced to overrule his reason, nay overbeare it, by giveing scope to his lycencious eye, first to see, then to delight in, lastly to covett a chaste beautie? Alas how many swarmes of dependantę, beeing creatures to his greatenes, will not only tell him, mocke him, and harden him in a redie & pregnant deceipte, that their loue is courtely and women were in their creation ordeyned to bee wooed, and to bee won; but also . . . (f. 166ᵛ).

It is not *their* love that is in question, but love, generally. 'Their' is a telling mistake, which shows that the writer of the manuscript did not understand what he was copying.

I can only suggest again that one must take such errors into consideration before accepting the two manuscripts as being in Ford's own hand.

Glancing now at these non-dramatic works together, one sees that the rapid improvement in the versification (if Ford indeed wrote *Christes Bloodie Sweat*) gives some promise of the poetry of, say, *'Tis Pitty*; and the interest in questions of conscience and psychology can be seen in retrospect as a preliminary to the analytical skill of the plays. But *The Golden Meane* and *A Line of Life* are commonplace in thought and not very distinguished in expression; Ford's prose here bears as little relation to the prose of D'avolos in *Loves Sacrifice* as does most non-dramatic Elizabethan prose to that written to be spoken on the stage (I think it was Mr Somerset Maugham who said we should not regret the absence of Shakespeare's prefaces: if we had them, they might be as contorted as *Euphues*).

From one error at least a reading of the non-dramatic work will save us: we shall not prattle about Ford's approval of passion and incest once we have found his own sentiments in *A Line of Life*:

In short to bee a man, the first branche of Resolution, is to knowe, feele, and moderate affections, w^ch like traytours and disturbers of peace, rise vp, to alter & quite chaunge the lawes of Reason; by working in the feeble, and oftentimes the sounder partes, an innovation of ffolly: hee can seeldome bee a florishing member of a body polliticke, and so a deserving publique man, but more rarely (scantly ever) a reconcilour of divisions, and soe a civill good man, for others y^t begins not betymes to discharge his owne dutie to himself. The proverbe was (and it is lamentable to speake with truth and say it is) that a man is a beast to a man; but it must bee of a necessitie grannted, when a man to himself is a monster, or more prouerbially a divell. (f. 152^v)

But of the dramatic genius there is practically no sign; and this fact alone may suggest—if a paradox may be permitted—how purely dramatic Ford's genius was. There is a kind of writer (Cyril Tourneur is another example) who expresses himself best when he is putting words into the mouths of others. He writes most convincingly and with most conviction when he is not personally involved. Such a man is likely to be an unsuccessful lyrist; he is a born dramatist. What Ford's non-dramatic work may, then, best suggest to us is that we may be on doubly dangerous ground if we seek personal expression of any direct kind in his plays. And we shall not be unduly surprised if we find the level of his art immeasurably higher as soon as he begins to write for the theatre.

# III

## THE PLAYS WRITTEN IN COLLABORATION

THE FIRST play in connection with which Ford's name is mentioned is *An ill beginning has a good end, & a bad beginning may have a good end.* (I say the first, because there is no reason to doubt the identification of it with *A bad beginning makes a good end*, acted in 1613.) *An ill beginning*, with three other non-extant plays, *Beauty in a Trance, The Royall Combate* and *The London Merchant*, was attributed to Ford by Moseley when entering them on the Stationers' Register (*Beauty in a Trance* in September 1653, the others in June 1660). Warburton also listed them among the plays burnt by his cook.

Professor T. M. Parrott has shown[1] that *An ill beginning* is most unlikely to have been by Ford, who does not appear again as a dramatist, even as a collaborator, until 1621; and Sir Edmund Chambers has suggested that *The London Merchant* might be the result of confusion with *The Bristowe Merchant*, written by Ford and Dekker.[2] Beyond noting that *Beauty in a Trance* was called by Warburton a comedy, was performed in 1630, and was protected against piracy, with other plays belonging to the King's Men, in 1641,[3] and that the other three were described by Moseley as comedies, it seems best to leave these four plays out of further consideration. Nobody could now say that the evidence for Ford's authorship—even for the existence of two of them—is strong.

The plays in which Ford may have collaborated in his next period may now be listed as follows:

1621 *The Witch of Edmonton* (with Dekker and Rowley)
1622–3 *The Spanish Gipsie* (published as by Middleton and Rowley)
1623? *The Welsh Embassador* (probably mainly by Dekker)
1624 *The Sun's-Darling* (with Dekker)

[1] *Modern Language Notes*, lxviii (April 1943), 247–53.
[2] *The Elizabethan Stage* (Oxford, 1923), iii. 316.
[3] G. E. Bentley: *The Jacobean and Caroline Stage* (Oxford, 1941). i. 28; see also p. 120.

1624  *The Fairy Knight* (with Dekker—the play is lost)

1624  *A Late Murther of the Sonn upon the Mother* (with Webster, Dekker and Rowley—lost)

1624  *The Bristowe Merchant* (with Dekker—lost)

1625  *The Faire Maide of the Inne* (licensed and first published as by Fletcher).

*The Duke of Lerma* is a special case; I shall treat it separately.

H. Dugdale Sykes and Miss Sargeaunt, particularly, have analysed Ford's share in the extant plays (with the exception of *The Welsh Embassador*). In their analyses, they have relied mainly on vocabulary tests (Sykes,[4] in particular, was sure that he could detect Ford by these) and on the presence of certain dialectal peculiarities which are a feature of Ford's work, such as the use of the abbreviations 'd'ee' and 't'ee' even in serious dialogue and the pronunciation of words like 'girl' and 'pearl' as dissyllables. These dialectal peculiarities, although not confined to Ford, do provide unusually strong evidence of his hand when one is apportioning work written in collaboration. On the whole, it is difficult to quarrel with the attributions generally accepted; but there are certain reservations to be made.

My own impression is that, if anything, Ford's share in *The Witch of Edmonton* has been exaggerated. The play, which was not published until 1658, may be confidently dated 1621, between the publication of its pamphlet source, *The Wonderfull Discoverie of Elizabeth Sawyer A Witch Late of Edmonton* (by Henry Goodcole) and its production at Whitehall on 29 December. The elaborate title-page gives, in its opening phrases, such 'external' information as we have concerning the authors:

The Witch of Edmonton: A known true Story. Composed into A Tragi-Comedy By divers well-esteemed Poets; William Rowley, Thomas Dekker, John Ford, &c. Acted by the Princes Servants, often at the Cock-Pit in Drury-Lane, once at Court, with singular Applause. Never printed till now.

Many have endeavoured to allot shares in the play; Sykes summarizes all the important attempts up to his own day in the course of his analysis; and Miss Sargeaunt has since reviewed the evidence again.

[4]*Notes and Queries*, cli (1926), 435–8, 453–7.

Everyone agrees that I. i. is by Ford. Sykes—not given to underrating the value of stylistic parallels—could have added to his list such typical Ford constructions as

> presume you are
> A Debtor to your promise

and

> If you infect mine ear with any breath
> That is not throughly perfum'd with sighs
> For former deeds of lust . . .

although in fairness Miss Sargeaunt should have noted Frank's

> I have a suit t'ye

instead of the usual Ford 't'ee'.

The evidence for Ford in I. ii. is not strong, in spite of Gifford's ascription, supported by Fleay and Swinburne. Sykes finds only a few verbal parallels; I would say that even Miss Sargeaunt's assigning to him of the section after the entrance of Frank is debatable. Act II, scene i can be confidently given to Dekker and Rowley. If Ford wrote any of II. ii., I think it was only after the entrance of Frank and Susan; the only telling parallels Sykes finds are in that part of the scene. Act III scene i (Acts III and V are not divided in the Quarto—I give the modern divisions) is probably by Dekker and Rowley; III. ii. is Ford. The general similarity to Ford's style here has impressed all who have considered the play; and Sykes rightly stressed the similarity between the disguised Winnifride's grief when Susan calls Frank her husband:

> *Win.*　Oh Gods! Oh, mine eyes!
> *Sus.*　How now? what ailst thou, Lad?
> *Win.*　Something hit mine eye, it makes it water still,
> 　　　　Even as you said, *Commended to my Husband.*
> 　　　　Some door I think it was

and Flavia's famous line in *The Fancies Chast and Noble*

> Beshrew't, the brim of your hat
> Strucke in mine eye.　(III. 1269–70)

In Act III, scenes iii and iv and IV. i. there is very little evidence of Ford; Sykes's reason for assigning to him a share in III. iv. is particularly weak, and Miss Sargeaunt gives him credit for what is good in IV. i. solely because it is good. (I believe I have a

higher opinion of Dekker than have most who have written of
*The Witch of Edmonton*; and one might argue that Ford could
have used a restraining influence on his collaborator, if one did
feel the need to explain the unusual succinctness of the Dekker
parts of the play.) The main reason for giving Ford a share in
III. iii. is that it is so crucial to the part of the plot he was
developing (i.e. the Frank Thorney-Winnifride section); the
single verbal parallel is not convincing, so that the only other
evidence of Ford's authorship might be found in the typical
paradox of Susan's gratitude for being stabbed (she has just
learnt that Frank was already married when he 'married' her):

> And I deserve it.
> I'm glad my fate was so intelligent.
> 'Twas some good Spirits motion. Die? Oh, 'twas time!
> How many yeers might I have slept in sin?
> Sin of my most hatred too, Adultery?

Act IV scene ii is more likely to have been written by Ford. It
is the scene of Frank's arrest, and Sykes finds a few parallels,
but the argument is not fully convincing. There is no sign of
Ford in v. i.; but his hand can be detected in v. ii., in which he
would again need to take part to round off the Frank-Winnifride
story. Warbeck and old Carter in this scene remind one, too,
in the dignity of their grief and in their situations, of Daliell and
Huntley in *Perkin Warbeck* (one has been passed over for another
lover, the other has lost a daughter, here by death).

For the purposes of literary criticism, it is clearly better, in
questions of collaborate work, to take the conservative view.
And I am all the more content to judge Ford on I. i., III. ii. and
v. ii. alone because I am convinced that adequate justice has not
yet been done them. They seem to me excellent—and from a
man writing possibly his first play, astounding.

Was Swinburne so far wrong when he claimed of the opening
scene of *The Witch of Edmonton*, in his Essay *John Ford*, 'there is
no more admirable exposition of a play on the English stage'?[5]
'Enter Frank Thorney, Winnifride *with-child*' says the stage-
direction, and Frank's opening speech gets to the point with
something of the suddenness of Webster's famous 'Banished!'
(*'Tis Pitty* shows that the art was remembered.)

---

[5] *Works*, Bonchurch edition, vol. 12 (Prose Works, vol. ii) p. 394.

> Come, Wench; why here's a business soon dispatch'd.
> Thy heart I know is now at ease: thou needst not
> Fear what the tattling Gossips in their cups
> Can speak against thy fame: thy childe shall know
> Who to call *Dad* now.

The dramatist proceeds to develop the character of Frank—jovial, plausible, but obviously unsound though not yet evil. Winnifride's real feeling for him is all the greater by contrast.

Frank has arranged for her to retire to her uncle's home near Waltham Abbey

> He'll use thee kindly: thou shalt want no pleasures,
> Nor any other fit supplies whatever
> Thou canst in heart desire. *Win.* All these are nothing
> Without your company. *Frank.* Which thou shalt have
> Once every month at least. *Win.* Once every month!
> Is this to have an Husband? *Frank.* Perhaps oftner:
> That's as occasion serves. *Win.* I, I, in case
> No other Beauty tempt your eye, whom you
> Like better, I may chance to be remembred,
> And see you now and then.

Frank vows that he will never

> falsifie that Bridal-Oath
> That bindes me thine. And, *Winnifride,* when ever
> The wanton heat of youth by subtle baits
> Of beauty, or what womans Art can practice,
> Draw me from onely loving thee; let Heaven
> Inflict upon my life some fearful ruine.

There is a kind of double irony here; Frank does 'falsify' the bridal-oath and Heaven does ruin him—but not because another woman has drawn him from loving Winnifride. He is to marry Susan because he is too weak to face the alternative and is to be executed for murdering her. And he murders her only that he may retain Winnifride.

There follows an interview between Frank and Sir Arthur Clarington—a battle of wits between two men neither of whom is entirely honest. Sir Arthur challenges Frank with disgracing Winnifride and not marrying her; Frank replies that marriage would bring both of them 'to beggery'; Sir Arthur offers a marriage portion; Frank accepts and then reveals that they are already married; and Sir Arthur is left alone for a fraction of a minute to drop the bombshell:

> Go thy way Cuckow; have I caught the young man?
> One trouble then is freed. He that will feast
> At others cost, must be a bold fac'd guest.

Winnifride enters and Sir Arthur is enthusiastic about her 'art'; he is shocked to learn that she intends to remain true to her husband:

> Wilt thou turn monster now? Art not asham'd
> After so many months to be honest at last?
> Away, away, fie on't.

One's mind leaps forward to that other superb surprise, Giovanni's response to the Friar's suggestion that Annabella should be married:

> Marriage? Why that's to dambe her; that's to proue
> Her greedy of variety of lust
>
> ('Tis Pitty, II. 946–7)

I can no more understand how critics can say that Ford lacks great single lines than I can understand the persistence of that other heresy begun, I believe, by Swinburne[6] that Ford owed little to Shakespeare. The debt will, I hope, be made apparent throughout this study. And here already in this opening scene of *The Witch of Edmonton* is a typical instance of Ford's deliberate echoing of his great predecessor.

Winnifride is unmoved by Sir Arthur's outburst; she will not allow him to ruin even by word

> A Temple hallowed to the purity
> Of holy Marriage.

She will remain with her uncle to await the birth of her child. And Sir Arthur's answer is

> Get you to your Nunnery,
> There freeze in your old Cloyster. This is fine.

The daring of the adaptation and the added force the line gets from the very contrast with the original Shakespearian situation must surely mark this use of 'literary allusion' as being at least as fine as anything the twentieth century has achieved.

In Act III, scene ii Frank has married Susan bigamously, to gain her dowry and because he is too weak to meet the trouble that would come from the revelation to his father of his marriage

---

[6]*Op. cit.*, pp. 371–2; cf. the statement that Ford was 'not, like Massinger and Shirley, full of echoes of Shakespeare, Webster, and Fletcher' (Schelling and Black, *Typical Elizabethan Plays*, New York, 1949, p. 900).

to Winnifride. He is satisfied to have Winnifride dress as a boy
and leave the country with him; he still cannot face facts and
tries to convince himself that his father's conduct forced the
situation on him. Winnifride's distress is beautifully conveyed,
first as she listens to him and then as she has to act her part
while Susan, believing herself to be his wife and taking
Winnifride for a page, assures her of Frank's respect and bids
her look after him:

> Thou maist be Servant, Friend, and Wife to him.
> A good Wife is then all.

Winnifride can only agree. The tragic irony of the situation
constantly mounts with such lines as Susan's

> I would thou hadst a womans bosom now

until Winnifride leaves the other two alone. Then Ford brings
out more fully the tragedy of Susan, whose grace, charm and
grief are contrasted with Frank's impatience to be gone

> What a Thorne this Rose grows on? parting were sweet.
> But what a trouble 'twill be to obtain it?

Act v, scene ii is almost certainly not wholly Ford but it seems
highly probable on all counts that he wrote the final speeches
of Frank, who in moving words expresses his repentance before
he is led to execution for the murder of Susan. Ford probably
also wrote such lines as Winnifride's refusal to be comforted:

> Comfort and I
> Are too far separated to be joyn'd
> But in eternity. I share too much of him that's going thither.

But the Witch sections here, as throughout the play, must be
Dekker's, and in such scenes, involving the different threads of
the plot, the collaboration must necessarily have been close.

The interesting fact we shall probably never know is just why
Ford was given the Frank-Winnifride section of the story. It
may, of course, have been sheer chance that led Dekker (or
whoever was dividing the play) to allot to Ford the kind of
tragic scene in which he was to show throughout his career his
greatest power; it is just possible that there was earlier dramatic
work in which he had shown his capabilities; it is certain that
there was nothing in his non-dramatic poetry and prose to
point to his success here. It remains probable that it was on

their knowledge of the man himself that the collaborators based
their choice. It was a sound one; and after *The Witch of Edmonton*
Ford naturally is given this type of work again.

If one chooses to regret that he did not serve his dramatic
apprenticeship with artists who placed greater stress on the connection of the different plots of a play, it is, I think, the only
regret that is left to a Ford admirer by *The Witch of Edmonton*.
We are not surprised to learn from Professor Bentley[7] that the
play was being revived as late as 1636.

There is no external evidence at all for attributing to Ford
*The Spanish Gipsie*. Both the early editions, that of Marriot in
1653 and that of 1661, name the authors as 'Thomas Midleton,
and William Rowley. Gent.' The attribution of the play to
Ford was made by Dugdale Sykes[8] and accepted, with the
elimination of the gipsy scenes, by Miss Sargeaunt. By both
critics the tests used are those that were applied to *The Witch
of Edmonton*.

The evidence is, however, both less convincing and harder to
interpret than in the other play. If Sykes's argument be closely
examined, it will, I believe, be clear that there is no real reason
for connecting Ford with Act I, scenes ii and iv (the scene
divisions are again not in the original quartos); Act II, both
scenes; Act III, scene ii; and Act IV, all three scenes. (Miss
Sargeaunt has suggested that the monosyllabic pronunciation
of 'girl' in II. i. is evidence against Ford's authorship of that
scene; and the word is again a monosyllable, I would add, in
II. ii. 'Yes Girle, thou dost'.) Of the remaining scenes, I. i. in
which Roderigo carries off Clara after brief conversation with
Lewys and Diego, is too slight to be attributed safely to any
playwright; in I. v. the phrases that suggest Ford's presence

> then draw to ebb
> The float of those desires
>     *I* unclaspe
> The secrets of my heart
>       court my studies now
> For Phisick 'gainst infection of the minde

and

---

[7] *Op cit.*, i. 251-2.
[8] *Modern Language Review*, xix (1924), 11-24—an article reprinted as chapter ix
of *Sidelights on Elizabethan Drama*.

> No friend but thou alone, for whose sake only
> I undertake this voluntary exile
> Shall be partaker of my griefes

cease with the entrance of Diego and departure of Roderigo,
i.e. after about seventy-three lines; in III. i. the only sign of Ford's
hand is in the opening soliloquy by Roderigo—twenty-nine or
thirty lines; and in v. ii. (another short scene) the 'evidence' for
Ford is one phrase:

> trust me I have wept
> Religiously to wash off from my Conscience
> The staine of my offence.

There remain only I. iii., III. iii., v. i. and v. iii. which do strongly
suggest Ford, but not, I think, all the time. On these four scenes
and the parts of scenes just defined, attention can be concentrated.

To the Ford-like phrases quoted by Sykes from I. iii. one
might add

> so with your Sword
> Let out that blood which is infected now,
> By your soule-staying lust.

This scene is the conversation of Roderigo and Clara immediately after the rape, and certainly has character interest. The
rapid changes of mood (not, surely, as Morris suggested in his
edition for the 'Belles-Lettres' series, the inconsistencies) of
Clara are skilfully shown. In turn, she asks Roderigo to kill her;
begs him to marry her; seizes him; and is shocked by his offer
of money:

> Gold, why! alas for what? the hire of pleasure,
> Perhaps is payment, mine is misery;
> I need no wages for a ruin'd name,
> More then a bleeding heart.

When she is left alone, she speaks to herself and thinks first of
revenge, but then she begins to take a practical interest in
her surroundings, noticing the moon, the room, the bed, the
window:

> Oh Heaven! the stars appeare 'too, ha! a chamber,
> A goodly one, dwells Rape in such a paradice!

One can understand why Sykes at first thought of Webster
('Looke you, the Starres shine still'?); but, if anything, the use

of the soliloquy for purposes of plot rather than character (Clara takes the crucifix that later enables her to identify her betrayer) is more characteristic of Middleton than of Ford. The rest of the scene, after Roderigo's return, does clearly suggest Ford; but I wonder whether Miss Sargeaunt does not claim too much for it and for later scenes when she speaks of Ford's study of the good influence on a man of a virtuous woman. Roderigo's request that he be now permitted to enjoy Clara 'with a free allowance' and his avowal that he means 'no second force' and grieves for his 'foule attempt'—these are not so very far above the level of the usual Elizabethan repentances and cannot really be compared with the study of Frank in *The Witch of Edmonton*.

In Act I, scene v Lewys, almost beside himself with grief because he has discovered that he has helped Roderigo carry off the woman he, Lewys, wishes to marry, asks what has happened to her but does not reveal her name. Roderigo tells of his repentance and Lewys hails him as 'The best man living'. (Yet later when Roderigo *marries* Clara, Lewys challenges him. There is something odd here.) Roderigo announces his intention of leaving the city.

In Act III, scene i Roderigo, in disguise, laments his situation—

A thousand stings are in me! oh what vild prisons
Make we our bodies, to our immortall souls!
Brave Tenants to bad houses!

—and begins to think of searching for the woman he has wronged.

Act III, scene iii is important particularly for the characterization of Clara. She has fainted and has been carried to Fernando's house, to the very room in which the rape took place. She recognizes it, and her grief is portrayed with dignity as she asks simple questions and is obviously moved by the replies.

*Clara.*              Yon large Window
    Yeilds some faire prospect, good my Lord looke out,
    And tell mee what you see there.
*Pedro.*              Easie suite,
    *Clara* it over-viewes a spacious Garden,
    Amidst which stands an Alablaster Fountaine,
    A goodly one.
*Clar.*             Indeed my Lord.

*Maria*                          The griefes grow wide,
And will mislead thy judgement through thy weakenesse
If thou obey thy weakenesse.
*Cla.*                          Who ownes these glorious buildings? . . .

Clara asks Fernando questions about his family, particularly his
son, and produces the crucifix

My Lord, d'ee know this Crucifix?

(The abbreviation 'd'ee' is one of the very few reasons for
suspecting Ford's hand in the scene.) When Fernando recognizes it, she is greatly moved:

Oh then I am a cast-away!

and she produces for Fernando a 'Paper' in which she has set
out her case. She asks not for vengeance but 'a noble satisfaction'; and Fernando eagerly agrees to help her to the satisfaction
she desires.

I cannot see Ford's hand at all in the somewhat pointless
Act IV, which includes the play within the play, and the incident
of Roderigo's being attracted to Clara who is in the audience
and is seen but not recognized by him. Fernando agrees to the
marriage. The plotting here is weak, and the long play within
the play has little to do with the sudden infatuation which
follows it.

Act V begins with startling 'turns' in the regular manner of
tragi-comedy. Fernando tells Roderigo that the woman he has
married is a wanton and demands to know what sin in his past
has brought such a punishment upon him. Roderigo's answer
is 'Rape'; and he can only lament:

Oh! had I married her,
I had been then the happiest man alive.

Clara reveals her identity and all are satisfied—except Lewys.

The remainder of the play deals with the unravelling of the
subplot and is chiefly memorable for the drawing of the character of Pretiosa, previously seen as a sprightly young gipsy girl
but now desperately earnest as she pleads for the life of her
lover, Don John (Andrew):

*Jo.*                  'Tis in vaine to storme;
My Fate is here determin'd!
*Pre.*                  Lost Creature,

> Art thou grown dull too; is my Love so cheape,
> That thou court'st thy destruction, 'cause I love thee?
> My Lords, my Lords; speake *Andrew*, prithee now,
> Be not so cruell to thy selfe and mee,
> One word of thine will doo't.

Very effective, too, is the restraint of her three-word reminder to Fernando in the final scene when Don John asks to be allowed to die if he may not have her.

> *Pre.* You promis'd mee.
> *Fer.* I did.

I have set all this out fully because it now seems necessary to say that although there are language clues, there is nothing in the characterization or plotting that seems particularly characteristic of Ford. I notice that Miss Sargeaunt thinks the characterization of Pretiosa (actually Fernando's daughter, Constanza, in disguise) beyond him—'Ford could hardly have touched in the picture with so light a hand' (p. 56); yet Pretiosa, in Act v scene iii, is one of the characters who use the abbreviation 'd'ee' that is said to identify Ford as the author! If the answer be that Ford was concerned with Pretiosa only incidentally and because she here comes momentarily into relationship with the Roderigo-Clara group, then one can only say that it is a very distant relationship and would imply a very arbitrary division of the play. Moreover it is in these later scenes that the character is most fully developed. The case for Ford begins to look weaker still.

*The Spanish Gipsie*, which was first licensed for acting in July 1623, was presumably still on the stage in 1639 when it was among the plays reserved by the Lord Chamberlain for the use of William Beeston's company;[9] it could then easily have been tinkered with or even revised between 1623 and publication in 1653. (*The Sun's-Darling* may be a parallel here.) I believe there are signs of dislocation: I have mentioned one such sign, the characterization of Lewys, and there is almost certainly another in Pedro's account to Lewys of the history of Alvarez, in II. ii.:

> His Wife the sister to the *Corigidor*,
> With a young Daughter, and some few that follow'd her . . .

This can only be taken by Lewys and the audience to mean the

[9] Bentley, i. 330–1.

daughter of Alvarez and his wife; but she was in fact the daughter of Fernando. There is no point whatever in the deception as it stands, and the audience has to make an unnecessary adjustment when it learns the truth.

Add to all this that Marriot's attribution of a play by the practically unknown Glapthorne to George Chapman, which is used by both Sykes and Miss Sargeaunt as proof that his attribution of *The Spanish Gipsie* cannot be trusted, is a very different matter from an attribution of a play by Ford to Middleton and Rowley—in which there would be no point. Then add, as Professor Ellis-Fermor has pointed out,[10] that the situation of Clara in the play is very like that of Bianca in *Women Beware Women*; remember that Middleton, the chameleon dramatist if ever there was one, is always likely to imitate someone else's style perfectly; note that the versification and methods of characterization in *The Spanish Gipsie* are nowhere unlike Middleton[11]—and I question very much whether you can do more than say that Ford at some stage of the play's history probably 'had something to do' with it. Like Professor Ellis-Fermor, though mainly for independent reasons, 'I am not yet prepared to see in this study more than Ford's hand alongside Middleton's'.[12]

It would seem, then, that in 1621 and the next few years, Ford was beginning to collaborate, probably at their invitation, with professional playwrights like Dekker and Middleton. His share in any play was not likely to be large; his assistance would probably be called for most often when a play of topical interest (such as *The Witch of Edmonton* or *A Late Murther*) had to be written rapidly; and, once he had shown his power, he would almost certainly be allotted, within limits, the parts of the plot likely to suit his already well-developed interest in human nature under stress.

The anonymous tragi-comedy *The Welsh Embassador*, which from a reference in the last act has been dated, fairly confidently, 1623, may well be another of the plays on which Ford worked

[10]*Jacobean Drama*, p. 142, note 2.
[11]Even the comic scenes are not unlike him. See W. D. Dunkel, 'Did not Rowley merely revise Middleton?', *Publications of the Modern Language Association*, xlviii (1933), 799–805.
[12]*Jacobean Drama*, p. 151, note.

with Dekker. It survives in a manuscript in the Cardiff Public
Library (the writing of which, it had better be stated now, is not
that of *Fames Memoriall* or *A Line of Life*) and has been edited for
the Malone Society by H. Littledale and W. W. Greg. The
attribution to Dekker is made in a list of his plays compiled
about 1678 by Abraham Hill[13] and is supported by parallels of
style listed in an article found among Bertram Lloyd's papers
after his death and published in the *Review of English Studies*.[14]

In the same article Lloyd gave reasons for thinking that two
scenes, III. iii. and v. i., were by Ford. He quotes some Ford-like
phrases, notes 'dee' and 'tee' each used at least twice (instead of
'd'ye' and t'ye') and thinks that the second of these scenes is
almost the only one in the play 'with any psychological handling'.

I see no reason for rejecting any of these suggestions. The
stylistic evidence is interesting and I would add that the lines
in which the King begins to regret his lustfulness and cruelty
have a characteristic Ford use of 'plurisie':

> trew bewty dwells in meeknes, loue w[th] pitty
> keepes leagues, there is a plurisie w[th]in mee
> requires a skillful surgion that can launce it.

There are no signs of Ford that I can detect elsewhere in the
play; and the two scenes are not altogether unworthy of
him.

The play as a whole is certainly poor enough. It is the story
of Athelstane, King of England, who, in spite of his written
contract to marry Armante, mother of his son, wishes to marry
Carintha, wife of Penda, son of the Duke of Cornwall, and
arranges to have Penda murdered.

In the first of the scenes attributed to Ford, III. iii., Carintha,
who has just learnt of the marriage contract, is visited by
Armante and her son, asking for pity. Carintha returns the

[13](a) Dr Greg is made to say 'Hall' (*R.E.S.*, xxi (1945), 201, note 3) but I think
this must be a misprint.
   (b) Dekker is also given in the Stationers' Register as the author of *The Noble
Soldier* of which *The Welsh Embassador* would seem to be little better than a
reworking. See Bertram Lloyd, 'Two Notes on Elizabethan Orthography',
*R.E.S.*, ii (1926), 204–6.
[14]Vol. xxi (1945), 192–201. Lloyd's notes have not always been set out correctly.
In the section marked 'Act I, sc. ii' he also quotes from I. iii. and in that marked
'Act II, sc. ii' he also quotes from II. i.

stolen contract to Armante, with the assurance that her own seeming willingness to marry the King is only part of a plan to awaken him 'out of this dreame'. The young Prince, not quite as precocious as some other Elizabethan children, has a few pathetic lines, and the emotion of the two women is adequately suggested; but there is hardly more characterization than this, the scene being important mainly in the development of the plan to cure the King.

Act v. scene i shows its culmination. The Prince is brought to the King, together with the information, actually false, that Armante has become a nun. Some of the subsequent lines are unfortunately mutilated, but again there is pathos in the boy's speeches:

> if cause my blood is yo$^r$s
> yo$^u$ thinck my life may bee some danger 'tee
> or that my mother in law, next yo$^u$ marry
> Cannot abide mee; yett Ile doe the best
> I can to please her, but theis stepmothers
> they saie doe seldome loue their husbandɇ children.

Pathos of this kind can quickly lose its effect and perhaps there is too much of it here. The mood changes, however, with the entrance of Carintha and her assumed anger at being 'made a goodlie foole' by the boy's presence. After her departure, the mood reverts to the original one, when the boy is brought back and cross-examined by his father about his mother's teachings. His answers complete the King's change of heart—and if this change lacks full credibility, that is largely because the King has been only a type figure in the earlier part of the play. The remainder of the scene, including the King's testing of the faithful Voltimar by the request that he kill the boy, is mostly conventional and lets the action down again to the level of the final two scenes of clarification and rejoicing.

The whole play gives me the impression of being incomplete—either mutilated or perhaps not fully restored. There may, then, be more significance than Lloyd thought in the fact that Henslowe had paid Dekker and Drayton in October 1598 for a play *Connan Prince of Cornwall* (Penda in *The Welsh Embassador* is son to the Duke of Cornwall and assumes the name of Conon). Did Ford alone or Ford and Dekker in collaboration perhaps set out to revise an earlier play of which Dekker had written at least part?[15]

That could be what happened with *The Sun's-Darling*. This play was licensed on 3 March 1624 by Herbert, whose entry reads 'For the Cockpit Company; *The Sun's Darling*; in the nature of a masque by Deker, and Forde'. It was not published until 1656, when the actors Theophilus Bird and Andrew Penneycuicke brought it out as '*The Sun's-Darling*: A Moral Masque: As it hath been often presented at Whitehall, by their Majesties Servants; and after at the Cock-pit in Drury Lane, with great Applause. Written by *John Foard* and *Tho. Decker* Gent.' (Professor Bentley suggests that Bird may even have been a friend of Ford's, since two prologues and a dedication for plays in whole or in part by Ford are signed by him.)[16]

The play has aroused little enthusiasm. A typical comment would be Miss Sargeaunt's:

Viewed as a whole *The Sun's Darling* is of little value as a work of art. It is not quite either a play or a masque, and could never succeed on the stage. The plot as it stands lacks real coherence, and the characters fall between two stools, as they are neither completely allegorical nor have any interest as real persons. (p. 63)

But whatever doubts may be raised by a slight alteration in the title-page for a reissue in 1657 ('As it hath been often presented by their Majesties Servants; at the Cock-Pit in Drury Lane, with great Applause'), the dedication, which Miss Sargeaunt overlooks, makes it quite clear that the play was in fact popular both in the public theatre and at Court; and it was among the plays protected by the Lord Chamberlain for Beeston's Boys in 1639. As Gifford suggested in his introductory note to the play, 'its activity and bustle, its May-games, its songs, and its dances' would have appealed.[17] Judged as 'straight' drama, no doubt, it has weaknesses; but such a play

[15]I note that J. Quincy Adams, writing before Ford's name was connected with *The Welsh Embassador*, thought the play was probably composed about 1600 and revised in 1623. ('Hill's List of Early Plays in Manuscript', *The Library*, xx. (1939), 86–8.)

[16]Op. cit., ii, 378. It may also be worth noting that different copies of this 1656 edition of *The Sun's-Darling* have the one dedication addressed to at least four different patrons. See an article by Professor F. P. Wilson in *Adams Memorial Studies* ed. J. G. McManaway *et al.* (Folger Shakespeare Library, Washington, 1948), p. 558.

[17]*The Dramatic Works of John Ford*, ed. W. Gifford, rev. A. Dyce and A. H. Bullen (London, 1895), iii. 102.

is seen in better perspective if one reflects that the moral-masque must have borne much the same relation to the straight drama of its day as the modern musical comedy bears to the drama proper in ours. In the moral-masque as in musical comedy the entertainment lies in what is given on the stage at any one moment; and continuity and consistency are relatively un-important.

*The Sun's-Darling*, which shows clear signs of the influence of Ben Jonson, has the usual masque kind of story and provides further evidence of the way in which types of Morality con-tinued alongside realistic drama, which never completely super-seded them. Raybright, the kinsman and 'Darling' of the Sun, is given his wish to be allowed to enjoy for one year

> the several pleasures here
> Which[18] every season in his kinde
> Can bless a mortal with.

He is entertained in turn by each of the four seasons (beginning with spring, one to each of the Acts II–V); and the interest of the modern audience flags because, as in all such plays, it does not find the entertainments as enthralling as the plot demands that they should be found. Raybright vows that he will stay with each of the seasons, but his squire Folly and his mistress Humour (in the Jonsonian sense) constantly lead him away. He finally realizes his mistake, and the Sun somewhat unnecessarily ex-plains the allegory and points the moral, that man continually

> puts off the minute
> Of resolution, which should bid farewel
> To a vain world of wearinesse and sorrows.

Even within these allegorical limits, however, the characteri-zation is not consistent. The original intention probably was to have Raybright become gradually more serious; but as the play stands there is merely a sudden wrench when in Act V he is hailed as the personification of the Just Prince:

> A Prince who is so excellently good,
> His virtue is his honor, more then blood;
> In whose clear nature, as two Suns, do rise
> The attributes of Merciful, and Wise.

It certainly seems that there was a change for some special

---

[18]The actual reading is 'with', an obvious error.

occasion that called for compliment, probably, as has been
suggested, to Charles I; I think there are signs that the courtiers
may even have participated as the masquers in Act v.

But are we to blame Ford for the sudden change? It was
easier to do so when it was confidently asserted that *The Sun's-
Darling* was a revision of Dekker's *Phaeton*, written in 1598 (and
altered for Court performance in 1600). But Sir Edmund
Chambers was never convinced[19] and W. L. Halstead has since
shown, in an article that has been overlooked by most Ford
scholars,[20] that there is nothing to be said for the identification
and a great deal to be said against it. It is impossible, then,
simply to assume that Ford was revising Dekker (and there was
always the possibility that Dekker helped with any such
revision). We are thrown back on internal evidence—and on
that alone I question whether anyone would ever have suspected Ford's hand at all. F. E. Pierce made a valiant attempt
to divide the play between the two dramatists; but his study,
'The Collaboration of Ford and Dekker'[21] only proved how few
are the similarities, even in Act v, with Ford's other work.

Pierce gave Dekker Acts II and III, Ford I, IV and v (with modi-
fications)—a division that has been accepted by all who have
analysed the play, except that Sykes for reasons which he did
not set out, gave Ford III. ii. Miss Sargeaunt, agreeing and
pointing out that 'girle' is monosyllabic in Act II and in III. iii.,
suggests that 'the freshness and gaiety of Act II are unmistakably
Dekker's' (p. 59). Yet Gifford and Pierce note that the rare
'smickly' in Act II suggests Ford, who uses 'smicker' in *Fames
Memoriall*; and I do not know of any better parallels in Acts I and
IV which are generally given to Ford without question. Moreover, if Raybright's ignorance of Folly's name in Act II,
although he has been told it in Act I, is taken as evidence that
one dramatist wrote Act I, the other Act II, then the similar
inconsistency within Act II (also pointed out by Gifford) when
Raybright announces that he has often heard Humour's praises
sung, although only a few lines before he seems to say that he
has never heard of her, would have to be taken as proof of
divided authorship there. Again, Pierce notes parallels to

[19]*Elizabethan Stage*, iii. 300.
[20]'Dekker's *Phaethon*', *Notes and Queries*, clxxv (1938), 380–5.
[21]*Anglia*, xxxvi (1912), 140–68.

Dekker's other work in Acts I and IV which for other reasons (mainly versification) he gives to Ford. I do not see any hope of making a satisfactory division with this evidence.

That the play was revised is highly probable—but in 1638 or 1639. I do not think sufficient attention has been paid to W. W. Lawrence's evidence that the opening pages of Act V are appropriate only to the relations of England and Scotland at that time.[22] If, then, anyone wishes to believe that Ford, as the surviving one of the two collaborators who wrote the play in 1624, was called in to alter Act V in 1639 as a compliment to Charles I, he is welcome to do so—but that is a very different matter from an assertion that Ford's part in the play was the rewriting of Acts I, IV and V in 1624 and that he therefore spoilt Dekker's original dainty masque of 1598. My own opinion is that Ford's share in 1624 was slight, perhaps no greater than his share in *The Welsh Embassador* a year before; with a 1639 revision probably between us and the original Ford-Dekker collaboration, finality seems impossible.

It will be remembered also that it is in Act II of *The Sun's-Darling* that is found the song:

> *What bird so sings, yet so does wail?*
> *'Tis Philomel the Nightingale*

which is better known as it appears in Blount's 1632 edition of Lyly's *Six Court Comedies*, in *Alexander and Campaspe*:

> *What Bird so sings, yet so dos wayle?*
> *O, t'is the ravish'd Nightingale.*

This song (like all the others in Lyly's plays, except two from *The Woman in the Moon*) does not appear in the earlier editions; it is therefore often said that it is by Dekker, written between the date of the composition of Lyly's plays and 1632, perhaps for *The Sun's-Darling*—and the argument has been extended to the other songs in Lyly's comedies. But although much has been written on the problem,[23] it remains unsolved and one certainly cannot rule out the possibility that Lyly wrote the songs himself and that the authors of the miscellany *The Sun's-Darling* were therefore introducing a popular favourite (and perhaps spoiling

---

[22] *The Times Literary Supplement*, 20 December 1923, p. 894.
[23] To the notes and articles listed in the *Cambridge Bibliography*, i, 505 may now be added Miss Dodds's note in the *T.L.S.*, 28 June 1941.

it in the process). If that is so, the other songs in *The Sun's-
Darling* could also be borrowings, composed by neither Ford
nor Dekker. In the circumstances, I should not care to venture
a confident opinion on Ford's authorship of the songs in the
play, although it may be granted that Folly's song in Act I
could easily be his.

Parrott and Ball say of 'this charming dramatic poem' which
'is a pageant rather than a play' that 'it is pleasant to find in the
Dekker scenes of this, his last known work for the stage, a late
flowering of his happy humour and his lilting lyric'.[24] With the
reservations made above, one may accept this; but of Ford the
play tells us little except that he was willing apparently to collaborate sometimes in work that was far removed from his usual
interests. Of his unaided plays, only *The Lovers Melancholy* could
be said to owe much to the masque tradition or technique.

Of *The Fairy Knight* we know only that it was licensed by
Herbert on 11 June 1624, probably for the Prince's Company,
as 'A new play, called, *The Fairy Knight*: Written by Forde, and
Decker'; and of *The Bristowe Merchant* that it was licensed on
22 October 1624: 'For the Palsgrave's Company; A new Play,
called, *The Bristowe Merchant*: Written by Forde, and Decker'.[25]

Of *A Late Murther of the Sonn upon the Mother* we know not only
that it was licensed in September 1624, as 'A new Tragedy,
called, *A Late Murther of the Sonn upon the Mother*: Written by
Forde, and Webster', but also all that Professor C. J. Sisson has
taught us.[26]

It appears that the play, which was acted at the Red Bull,
probably by Prince Charles's Company, was based on two real-
life episodes, the murder by Nathaniel Tindall of his mother on
9 April 1624 in Whitechapel, and the marriage of Tobias
Audley to the wealthy widow Anne Elsdon, while she was
intoxicated, with true Elizabethan revelry before and after, on
23 July of the same year. The only connection between the two
episodes was that Audley and Tindall were brought from New-
gate for trial, the one for felony and the other for murder, at
the same Gaol Delivery, on 3 September.

[24]*A Short View of Elizabethan Drama* (New York, 1943), p. 113.
[25]Bentley, i. 214, 156.
[26]'*Keep the Widow Waking*. A Lost Play by Dekker', *The Library*, 4th Ser., vol. viii,
1927, revised for *Lost Plays of Shakespeare's Age* (Cambridge, 1936).

Anne Elsdon's relatives, having tried in vain other forms of redress, alleged conspiracy to defame her; and it was largely from the surviving documents in this suit, in the Court of Star Chamber, that Professor Sisson was able to reconstruct the play. Dekker and Rowley were among those cited; Rowley died before he could be examined, but Dekker's deposition was taken on 24 March 1626.

In it he testifies that the play, which he calls '*The Late Murder in White Chappell*, or *Keepe the Widow Waking*' and which is generally called in the legal documents by the second name, was written by Webster, Rowley, Ford and himself, 'vppon the instructions giuen them by one Raph Savage'. His own part, he says, consisted of 'two sheetes of paper conteyning the first Act . . ., and a speech in the Last Scene of the Last Act of the Boy who had killed his mother'. The parts of the others are not specified, but Professor Sisson points out that the information given by Dekker is enough to show that the play was not divided as Elizabethan plays are usually supposed to have been divided, with one writer taking the main plot, another the subplot. This warning Miss Sargeaunt neglects when she asserts more than once, on no evidence known to me, that 'the murder plot was really the property of Ford and Webster' (p. 34). The licensing of the play as by Ford and Webster means probably, as again Professor Sisson has suggested, that their names came first in a list of authors which Herbert cut short.

Again, therefore, Ford is found collaborating in a play of which he was in no sense the originator; he was apparently called in by Dekker to write a part which was defined for him. In these ways, as in being founded on a real-life story of topical interest, *A Late Murther* is clearly comparable to *The Witch of Edmonton*—and the comparison may suggest how regrettable it is that the later play has been lost. Yet, had it survived, we might still have found difficulty in identifying Ford's part; although Dekker does not say that he himself worked over the play as a whole, it is not unlikely that he would have done so if only to make the necessary joins; and if Dekker could write a single speech for a scene, one could never be certain that a scene showing signs of Ford's hand was not in part by Dekker or another of the collaborators.

It is not surprising, then, that the other play in which Ford seems to have collaborated, *The Faire Maide of the Inne*, should prove difficult to divide. This tragi-comedy, probably written in 1625, was licensed as by Fletcher, on 22 January 1626, and was first published in the 1647 Beaumont and Fletcher Folio. I find it unwise, therefore, to disregard Fletcher as a probable collaborator, although most who have examined the play seem to eliminate him.

Earlier discussions are summarized by Mr F. L. Lucas in his edition of Webster. Mr Lucas's conclusions[27] are that the play was probably divided as follows:

    I.      Massinger
    II.     Webster
    III. i.  Ford, Webster?, Massinger
    III. ii. Ford, Massinger?, Webster
    IV. i.   Ford
    IV. ii.–v. ii. Webster
    v. iii.  Massinger, Webster

(Miss Sargeaunt simply disregards III. i. and ii. in her discussion.)

My own examination of the play leads me to agree that Ford's share cannot be *greater* than this. Whoever the other collaborators were, Ford's part seems to have been allotted to him (perhaps, as Mr Lucas suggests, Massinger's was the guiding hand); and neither imagery nor general phrasing suggests that Ford helped extensively except in these three scenes. This means that he did not carry the Cesario-Bianca story through the play: it is referred to in I. i. and II. ii; there is an important development in IV. ii. after Ford's share seems to have ended; and the story is not concluded until v. iii. But I do notice that although Bianca is on the stage for some time in IV. ii. before the entrance of Cesario, she says only a dozen words; her subsequent interview with Cesario (this is apparently by Webster) is remarkably brief; and in the final scene, v. iii., she and Cesario say practically nothing. This does look like an understanding between the collaborators that although they should each carry on the plot, none of them except Ford should treat Bianca fully

[27] *The Complete Works of John Webster* (London, 1927), iv. 152.

enough to introduce the possibility of inconsistency of characterization. Cesario—one of the most unpleasant young men in
all seventeenth-century drama—has been so well defined by
Massinger (if it was he) in Act I that anybody could have
carried on *his* story.

If Ford, then, had a share in III. i., it was probably primarily
because Bianca was concerned. But it is the Host and Forobosco
(the main comic character) who use the characteristic 't'ee' and
'd'ee', the second time (line 92) after an exchange between
Forobosco and the Clowne which is almost certainly Webster's.
The use of these abbreviations by comic characters is not
peculiar to Ford; but then it is Forobosco who also uses the
Ford-like 'an injury to sweetnesse' (line 103). Yet in the
speeches of Bianca and Cesario towards the end of the scene—
where one would expect Ford—there are no significant verbal
parallels. Cesario wants Bianca to 'love' him (not because he
misunderstands her character, as Miss Sargeaunt implies, but
rather because he is simply that sort of man!); and Bianca
proves his match:

> Cesar.                    love, *Bianca*,
> Is that firme knot which tyes two hearts in one,
> Shall ours be tyed so?
> Bian.                    Use a plainer word,
> My Lord. Instead of tyes, say marries hearts,
> Then I may understand.[28]

Ford could have written this; but there is no evidence to show
that he wrote it. In fact, the transitions from prose to verse are
odd throughout the scene; perhaps there was some amalgama-
tion of parts or possibly Ford worked over the whole scene
because Bianca was involved in part of it.

Mr Lucas apparently had Dugdale Sykes's manuscript notes
as his warrant for saying there are 'a certain number of verbal
parallels' to Ford in III. ii. He quotes only two such parallels
and supports the claim for Ford on metrical grounds. I could
add that 'Deputed Pilot for the Common-wealth' in line 10
suggests Ford, who usually speaks of a Commonwealth instead
of a state or country and often spells the word with the hyphen.
But I have searched in vain for stronger evidence; there are

---

[28] I quote this play from Lucas, vol. iv.

echoes of Webster and of Massinger; and it has been noted often that this scene of formal judgment (Cesario's mother Mariana disowns him as her son and is ordered by the Duke to marry him) is suggestive rather of *The Devil's Law-Case* than of any play by either Ford or Massinger. It would be folly, then, to quote from III. ii. to illustrate Ford's dramatic art.

A much stronger case has been made out by both Mr Lucas and Miss Sargeaunt for IV. i. 'An injury to gratfulnesse' (line 8), 'injury and infamy—To goodnes, To time and vertuous mention' (line 173), 'd'ee' and 't'ee' (four times) and the dissyllabic 'girle' (line 168), together with the other verbal parallels listed by Mr Lucas (on p. 151) show that Ford must have been at least the main author of the scene; and it does him credit.

Cesario boisteriously congratulates himself on the riches that are now his because of the Duke's pronouncement that if Mariana refuses to marry him, he shall have three-quarters of her wealth. Bianca comes to him in quite a different mood (the contrast reminds one of Giovanni and Annabella at the beginning of Act II in *'Tis Pitty*). She had formerly thought her (supposedly) low birth made marriage to him impossible; now she comes willingly to tender him the first fruits of her heart, believing that Mariana's disowning of him has disgraced him

> And am content t'accept you for my husband,
> Now when you are at lowest.

As she tries to tell Cesario this, he continually interrupts her with unfeelingly jovial exclamations and comments, such as:

> I will love thee,
> My good good maid, if that can make thee happy,
> Better and better love thee

so that *her* situation becomes all the more tragic. Her offer, of course, is rejected and, worse, ridiculed:

> What counsaile urg'd thee on, tell me—thy Father
> My worshipfull smug Host? was't not he wench?
> Or mother Hostesse? ha?

She still manages to withdraw with dignity, and Cesario, quite unmoved, watches her go:

> Harmelesse Biancha!
> Unskild, what hansome toyes are maids to play with!
> How innocent! but I have other thoughts
> Of nobler meditation . . .

The remainder of the scene shows him rejected as husband both by Mariana and by his sister Clarissa whom he proposes as a substitute for Mariana, since if Mariana's disowning of him is sincere, Clarissa is no longer his sister in fact. He is shaken by the rejections but is unrepentant, and his last word is

I can but dye a Batchelor, thats the worst on't.

A Ford admirer might be forgiven for suggesting that had Ford finished the play, he would have done better than to marry Bianca to this man. But a moment's reflection shows that such unsatisfactory endings are found in Ford's unaided plays as well.

What, it remains to ask, was the value to him of this period of collaboration?

He was working with some of the foremost playwrights of his day, men who could rise to the heights, particularly of tragedy, when they chose and who to this extent were admirable models. He probably learnt much from them about tragic drama. But he was working with them when they were more concerned to produce a play in haste; he was writing mainly tragi-comedy (*The Witch of Edmonton* is the exception); and because he was merely collaborating and with better known and more experienced dramatists, he was not gaining much practice at careful plot-construction. (What he could learn and did not forget was the advantage of basing a plot on a real-life story.) It may also be noted that he does not seem to have taken a larger share in the later of these collaborate plays than in the earlier.

Beyond this it is difficult to generalize. Stylistic tests can never lead to final results when men are working in collaboration; it is too easy for them to imitate each other, unconsciously or deliberately (and the more noticeable the dialectal peculiarities of any one of them, the greater might be the temptation to echo him if one were working on the same section of the plot). Moreover it is a fact that not one of these plays was thought worthy of publication by any of the collaborators; the plays without exception are lost, remain in manuscript or were published after the closing of the theatres. Obviously it would be a mistake to base too many generalizations upon them.

It may well be that Ford's first unaided play was of an entirely different kind precisely because he did not wish to seem to rival his former collaborators.

## IV

## The Lovers Melancholy

THERE is no doubt that *The Lovers Melancholy* was the first play of Ford's unaided authorship to be licensed (it was licensed on 24 November 1628) and that it was the first to be published (it appeared in 1629.) But there has been some question whether it was the first written; and on the evidence of similarities in versification which distinguish *'Tis Pitty* and *Loves Sacrifice* from Ford's other work, and of a passage in the dedication of *'Tis Pitty*, Miss Sargeaunt and others have suggested that these two plays come first.

But stylistic evidence is notoriously unreliable in deciding dates of composition; style is likely to be determined by subject matter at least as much as by chronology. It has also often been noted that Ford slides from one style to another within a play. Nor do I doubt myself that Ford's description of *'Tis Pitty* to the Earl of Peterborough:

> Your Noble allowance of *These First Fruites* of my leasure in the Action, emboldens my confidence, of your as noble construction in this Presentment: especially since my Seruice must euer owe particular duty to your Fauours, by a particular Ingagement

means only that the play was the first product of a particular period of leisure following some special employment (*The Lovers Melancholy* is similarly called 'the account of some leisurable houres'); yet these words have been taken to mean that *'Tis Pitty* was Ford's first play and a chronology of all his work based on them.[1]

It does not seem to have been observed by those who have tried to date Ford's plays that *The Lovers Melancholy* and *The Broken Heart* (published in 1633), together with the lost *Beauty in a Trance* (acted in 1630) belonged to the King's Men, whereas *Loves Sacrifice* and *'Tis Pitty* (both published in 1633), *Perkin Warbeck* (1634) and *The Fancies Chast and Noble* (1638) were all, as the title-pages tell us, performed by the Queen's Majesty's

[1]Compare Shakespeare's description of *Venus and Adonis* (1593) as 'the first heir of my invention', meaning possibly his first work to be published. He had certainly already written plays.

Servants at the Phoenix. Then *The Ladies Triall* was licensed to
Beeston's Boys in 1638.

Add to this (a) that there is a probable reference to *The Broken
Heart* in William Hemminge's *Elegy on Randolph's Finger* which
was written no later than 1632 and possibly as early as 1630:

> More worthyes Like to thes I could Impart
> but that wee are troubled w^th a broken hart[2]

(b) that the reference in *The Broken Heart*, IV. 1818, to Thomas
Deloney's *Garland of Good Will* would naturally suggest 1631,
when that work was published, though perhaps not for the first
time;

(c) that it has been suggested by Sherman[3] that Ford wrote *'Tis
Pitty* in or shortly after 1631, when the punishment of Sir Giles
Allington and Dorothy Dalton for their incestuous marriage had
aroused interest in the subject (and this would be in accord with
the practice of his days of collaboration);

(d) that Fleay could be right in his conjecture (mentioned and
dismissed by Miss Sargeaunt[4]) that a line in *Loves Sacrifice*
(III. 1576).

> For that I ne're before saw women Anticks

was a reference to the French women who first played in London
in November 1632; and

(e) that Crashaw's famous couplet

> Thou cheat'st us *Ford,* mak'st one seem two by Art
> What is *Love's Sacrifice* but *the Broken Heart?*

surely implies that of the two *The Broken Heart* was the earlier.
I cannot understand why this has not been stressed before; it
rules out completely Miss Sargeaunt's dating of *Loves Sacrifice*
and *The Broken Heart.*

It would seem to me probable, then, that the order of composition was this:

| | |
|---|---|
| 1628 | *The Lovers Melancholy* |
| 1629–30 | *Beauty in a Trance* |
| 1631–2 | *The Broken Heart* |
| 1632–3 | *Loves Sacrifice* and *'Tis Pitty* |

[2]See Moore Smith's introduction and notes to his edition of the *Elegy.*
[3]Introduction to *''Tis Pity' and 'The Broken Heart'*, 'Belles-Lettres' series (Boston, 1915), p. xxxvi.
[4]*John Ford*, p. 24.

1633–4    *Perkin Warbeck*
1635–6    *The Fancies Chast and Noble*
1637–8    *The Ladies Triall.*

I am tempted to add that the anonymous play *The Queen*, published in 1653 by Alexander Goughe, a former King's Man, was probably the last of the plays written by Ford for that Company and an experiment in a less restrained style. It is certainly closest to *The Lovers Melancholy* in its use of Burton.[5]

I shall, then, treat the plays in this order and hope to show that it creates no difficulties in our understanding of the dramatist's development. I certainly think that the onus of proof is on those who would support the conventional dating of the plays, with '*Tis Pitty* preceding *The Broken Heart*; at the same time, my critical assessment of Ford's work, while quite consistent with my new dating of the plays, does not, I think, depend upon it.

*The Lovers Melancholy* was first published with a dedication 'To My Worthily Respected Friends, Nathaniel Finch, Iohn Ford, Esquires; Mr. Henry Blunt, Mr. Robert Ellice, and all the rest of the Noble Society of Grayes Inne' and with four sets of commendatory verses. The most interesting of these, by William Singleton, tells us that the play was popular with the discriminating ('By th'*Best* approu'd'); and it has remained a favourite with lovers of Ford.

It is, perhaps, not as dramatic as his later works; with its steady succession of set scenes, it retains something of a masque technique and, particularly, tone, even in its main plot, so that Professor Ellis-Fermor aptly terms it 'a play of moods' (p. 230). Others seem at times to criticize it for lacking attributes it does not claim to possess; and Dr Struble misses its true quality altogether when she summarizes it as 'on the whole an anaemic

[5]In *The Psychiatry of Robert Burton* (Columbia University Press, 1944, p. 118) Bergen Evans states that S. B. Ewing ('Burton, Ford and *Andromana*', *P.M.L.A.*, liv. (Dec. 1939), 1007–17) 'seeks to prove that Ford was the author of *Andromana*', a play written in 1642 or later and published as by J.S. in 1660. This is incorrect. What Mr Ewing said was that the attribution was tempting, because of a very similar use of Burton, but not tenable: 'the spelling, diction, and idioms are utterly unlike those of the known Ford plays...and there is not a scrap of external evidence that Ford wrote a play about Andromana'. What the poor play shows is that 'Ford was not without at least one follower in his own time', particularly in his use of Burton. I wholeheartedly support Mr Ewing and add that the versification and construction would alone rule out Ford as author. (*Andromana* may be found in Dodsley's *Old English Plays*.)

production' albeit 'rescued from being commonplace by really
beautiful verse and sensitive emotion'.[6] We shall see that the
characterization is by no means anaemic; and indeed a better
word to describe the play as a whole is 'academic'.

In a way, *The Lovers Melancholy* is an exercise in reworking
situations from earlier drama. It is certainly, as the Prologue
claims, a Scholar's play:

> To tell yee (Gentlemen) in what true sense
> The Writer, Actors, or the audience
> Should mold their Iudgemēts for a Play, might draw
> Truth into Rules, but we haue no such law.
> Our Writer, for himselfe would haue yee know,
> That in his following Sceanes, he doth not owe
> To others Fancies, nor hath layne in wait
> For any stolne Inuention, from whose height
> He might commend his owne, more then the right
> A Scholer claimes, may warrant for delight.
> It is Arts scorne, that some of late haue made
> The Noble vse of Poetry a Trade.
> For your parts (Gentlemen) to quite his paines,
> Yet you will please, that as you meet with straines
> Of lighter mixtures, but to cast your eye
> Rather vpon the maine, then on the bye.
> His hopes stand firme, and we shall find it true,
> The *Louers Melancholy* cur'd by you.

Ford would obviously like to think himself above writing for the
popular stage as a professional dramatist; and in his and
Massinger's continued protests that the comic parts of their
plays are only incidental and can be overlooked, there may well
be recognition of the fact that Court drama would find no place
for such frivolity.

The principal literary influence on Ford's play is, of course,
Burton. Ford acknowledges this when he inserts a marginal
note opposite Corax's exposition of Melancholy in Act III:
'Vid. Democrit. Iunior'; and scholars like S. Blaine Ewing[7] and
G. F. Sensabaugh[8] have made perhaps the principal contribution of America to Ford studies by demonstrating how extensive
is the dramatist's indebtedness to *The Anatomy of Melancholy*. Not

[6] *A Critical Edition of Ford's 'Perkin Warbeck'* (Univ. of Washington Press, Seattle,
1926), p. 10.
    [7] *Burtonian Melancholy in the Plays of John Ford* (Princeton, 1940).
    [8] *The Tragic Muse of John Ford* (Stanford, 1944).

only are the symptoms described and presented in Corax's masque of melancholics almost straight from Burton; but also most of the main characters in the play and many in Ford's other plays are described and analysed by reference to *The Anatomy*, which is used almost as a medical textbook.

What this means, I believe, is that Burton provided Ford with his terminology much as the new science provided Donne with his imagery. But it does not mean that Ford did not also draw from real life; it does not mean that his plots were predetermined by Burton; and it certainly does not rule out other influences on his characterization. The briefest glance at *The Lovers Melancholy* will suggest that Ford was deliberately recalling his dramatic predecessors. In making drama from the exposition of humours and the curing of them he must have owed something to Ben Jonson; Rhetias is a very Marstonian Malcontent, both in speech and in function, and the only reason for his soliloquy in Act III in which he deplores his life at Court is apparently that such characters generally had such soliloquies; and although the symptoms of Meleander's madness have been borrowed from Burton, Ford always keeps one eye firmly on Shakespeare. It may suffice to recall Lear's:

> Pray do not mocke me:
> I am a very foolish fond old man,
> Fourescore and vpward,
> Not an hour more, nor lesse:
> And to deale plainely,
> I feare I am not in my perfect mind
>
> (IV. viii. 59–63)

and compare Meleander's:

> My braines are dull'd;
> I am intranc'd, and know not what you meane:
> Great, gracious Sir, alas, why do you mocke me?
> I am a weake old man, so poore and feeble,
> That my vntoward ioynts can scarcely creepe
> Vnto the graue, where I must seeke my rest.
>
> (V. 2702–7)

The plot also owes much more to Shakespeare than to Burton.

Menaphon, son of Sophronos, returns from his travels which have been undertaken in an attempt to forget Thamasta. He brings with him the beautiful 'youth' Parthenophill, who is really Eroclea in disguise. Eroclea is the girl for whom

Thamasta's cousin, Prince Palador, is secretly pining and is
neglecting his state, Cyprus. (Palador seems to be the melancholy lover of the title, if one must be specified, which is doubt-
ful.) Eroclea's sister, Cleophila, is loved by Thamasta's brother
Amethus, the friend of Menaphon. There are, then, three pairs
of lovers—Menaphon and Thamasta, Palador and Eroclea,
Amethus and Cleophila—and the play is the story of the com-
plications which keep each pair of lovers apart until careful
contrivance finally brings them together again.

The first complication is the madness of Meleander, father of
Eroclea and Cleophila. It is the supposed loss of Eroclea which
has caused Meleander's mind to wander; and Cleophila conceives it her duty to stay with him. Accordingly when Amethus
seeks her hand, she can only reply:

> Sir, this for answer: If I euer thriue
> In an earthly happinesse, the next
> To my good Fathers wisht recouery,
> Must be my thankfulnesse to your great merit;
> Which I dare promise for the present time:
> You cannot vrge more from me.
>
> (II. 1110–15)

(I would suggest in passing that these lines show perfectly what
Singleton meant when he expressed the hope

> that the Age
> May be indebted to Thee, for Reprieue
> Of purer language.

Ford's beautifully clear—but not frigid!—diction is not the least
of his merits, and this as much as anything in his plots may be
his debt to Beaumont and Fletcher.)

The second complication in the plot is also Shakespearian,
rather than Fletcherian. Thamasta falls in love with the disguised Eroclea—the situation of *Twelfth Night* and *As You Like It*
—and because it is a borrowed situation Ford hardly troubles
to make Thamasta's infatuation probable. He also borrows
from *As You Like It* the further complication that Eroclea
promises to love Thamasta's waiting woman Kala if any woman:

> If euer I desire to thriue
> In womans fauour *Kala* is the first
> Whom my ambition shall bend to.
>
> (II. 910–912)

There may even be in Palador's famous lines

> *Rhetias*, thou are acquainted with my griefes,
> *Parthenophill* is lost, and I would see him;
> For he is like to some thing I remember
> A great while since, a long, long time agoe

a distant echo of the Duke's                    (IV. 2075–8)

> I do remember in this shepherd boy
> Some lively touches of my daughter's favour
> *(As You Like It,* v. iv. 26–7)

although of course nothing could be purer Ford than that characteristic repetition and falling cadence; cf.

> No hope liues then
> Of euer, euer seeing her againe
> (II. 761–2)

and

> a lamentable tale of things
> Done long agoe, and ill done (IV. 1938–9).

The whole situation of Eroclea's disguise as a youth is splendidly handled by Ford. Eroclea does her best to remain unnoticed; she answers politely any questions put to her but never says more than a few words and always tries to conceal her emotion. Typical is her restrained but pointed contribution to the discussion of Palador by Menaphon, Amethus and Thamasta:

*Men.*   His wonted melancholy still pursues him.
*Amet.*   I told you so.
*Tham.*   You must not wonder at it.
*Eroc.*   I doe not, Lady.                    (II. 861–5)

The cautious first approaches of Kala, sent by Thamasta, are received by Eroclea with dignity, but rejected except for the offer to choose Kala before any other woman. This offer is made in Thamasta's presence, and one notices immediately Ford's particular skill—in suggesting emotion not by words so much as by the absence of them. Thamasta's only comment is the cold

> Indeed.
> But say a Nobler Loue should interpose?
> (II. 914–15)

Eroclea's departure, however, is followed by an outburst against Kala; Ford is equally skilful in showing the almost undignified venom and rage of the normally proud and haughty Thamasta:

Art thou a Riuall fit to crosse my Fate?
Now pouerty and a dishonest fame,
The waiting-womans wages, be thy payment.
False, faithlesse, wanton beast, Ile spoile your carriage;
There's not a Page, a Groome, nay, not a Citizen
That shall be cast vpon yee. *Kala*,
Ile keepe thee in my seruice all thy life time,
Without hope of a husband or a suter.

(II. 936–43)

Granted Thamasta's love for Eroclea, then—and any inadequacy is in this original premise—the rest follows naturally.
And when Eroclea and Thamasta meet, the difference between
Ford's use of the conventional story of the woman in disguise
and Shakespeare's becomes apparent. Shakespeare is more or
less content to use it, in *Twelfth Night* and *As You Like It*, as a
convention, for its plot interest and its comic possibilities. Ford
explores the situation for its psychological interest and is not
afraid to investigate psychological abnormality if necessary.
There is surely more real passion in this scene in *The Lovers
Melancholy* than in the whole of *Twelfth Night*:

*Tham.*  Thou hast a moouing eloquence; *Parthenophill*,
　　　　*Parthenophill*, in vaine we striue to crosse
　　　　The destiny that guides vs. My great heart
　　　　Is stoopt so much beneath that wonted pride
　　　　That first disguiz'd it, that I now preferre
　　　　A miserable life with thee, before
　　　　All other earthly comforts.
*Eroc.*  *Menaphon*, by me, repeates the selfe-same words to you:
　　　　You are too cruell, if you can distrust
　　　　His truth, or my report.
*Tham.*  Goe where thou wilt,
　　　　Ile be an exile with thee, I will learne
　　　　To beare all change of fortunes.
*Eroc.*  For my friend, I pleade with grounds of reason.
*Tham.*  For thy loue,
　　　　Hard-hearted youth, I here renounce all thoughts
　　　　Of other hopes, of other intertainements,—
*Eroc.*  Stay, as you honour Vertue.
*Tham.*  When the proffers of other greatnesse—
*Eroc.*  Lady.
*Tham.*  When intreats of friends;—
*Eroc.*  Ile ease your griefe.
*Tham.*  Respect of kindred;
*Eroc.*  Pray giue me hearing.

*Tham.*  Losse of Fame;
*Eroc.*  I craue but some few minutes.
*Tham.*  Shall infringe my vowes, let Heauen—
*Eroc.*  My loue speake t'ee; heare then, goe on.
*Tham.*  Thy loue, why, tis a Charme to stop a vow
         In its most violent course.
*Eroc.*  *Cupid* has broke
         His Arrowes here; and like a child vnarm'd,
         Comes to make sport betweene vs with no weapon,
         But feathers stolne from his mothers Doues.
*Tham.*  This is meere trifling.
*Eroc.*  Lady, take a secret.
         I am as you are, in a lower ranke
         Else of the selfe samesexe, a maide, a virgine.
                                        (III. 1448–85)

Thamasta is left again almost without words, and can only beg
the favour of silence. To compare this scene with the earlier uses
of the situation in drama is like comparing with a Ben Jonson
love-lyric one by Donne. Ford does bring out what such a mis-
taken affection can mean to the person deceived; it is
Shakespeare, in comparison, who is merely 'pretty'.

Ford also shows the effect of the deception on the other
characters. Menaphon, having been placed by the injured Kala
where he can see the interview between Thamasta and Eroclea
but not hear it, afterwards speaks to the startled Thamasta with
well-nigh unforgivable violence; and Amethus, when he is told
of it, also insults her. Ford ably suggests the effect of all this on
Thamasta, who will never be so arrogant again. She is brought
'out of her humour' without any strain on probability at all.

Apart from the skill in characterization of this main plot,
three features of the play, particularly, should be commented on.
One is the drawing of Meleander, on whom Ford seems to have
lavished special care. The treatment of madness on the Elizabethan stage, outside Shakespeare, was not always sympathetic
and rarely pathetic. If Ford sometimes falls short of tragedy, he
does not often fail to achieve pathos; and his success is clear in
such speeches as Meleander's when he gazes on Eroclea's
picture as his reason returns:

> *Eroclea.* Tis the same, the cunning Artsman
> Faultred not in a line. Coo'd he haue fashen'd
> A little hollow space here, and blowne breath

To haue made it moue, and whisper, 't had bin excellent.
But faith, tis well, tis very well as tis.
Passing, most passing well.                    (v. 2548–53)

I am not underestimating the influence of Shakespeare on either
Ford or Shelley when I suggest that this is the kind of writing
that might well have led to some of Shelley's best lines in *The
Cenci*, such as

Give yourself no unnecessary pain,
My dear Lord Cardinal. Here, Mother, tie
My girdle for me, and bind up this hair
In any simple knot; ay, that does well.
And yours I see is coming down. How often
Have we done this for one another; now
We shall not do it any more. My Lord,
We are quite ready. Well, 'tis very well.
                            (v. iv. 158–65)

(Havelock Ellis points out[9] that Shelley's unfinished drama
*Charles I* is very like Ford in style.)

Meleander's speeches are not all in this mood. Equally in
character and also vivid is an earlier speech:

When I am dead,
Saue charge; let me be buried in a nooke.
No guns, no pompous whining: these are fooleries.
If whiles we liue, we stalke about the streets,
Iustled by Carmen, Foot-poasts, and fine Apes,
In silken coates, vnminded, and scarce thought on;
It is not comely to be hal'd to the earth,
Like high fed Iades vpon a Tilting-day,
In antique trappings: scorne to vse-lesse teares.
*Eroclea* was not coffind so: she perisht,
And no eye dropt saue mine, and I am childish.
                            (ii. 1076–86)

And both in the unexpected thought and in the simplicity of the
expression, Meleander's words when Eroclea reveals herself
approach great tragedy:

*Cleophila*, I thanke thee and the Prince,
I thanke thee too, *Eroclea*, that thou would'st
In pitie of my age, take so much paines
To liue, till I might once more looke vpon thee,
Before I broke my heart: O twas a piece
Of piety and duty vnexampled.        (v. 2571–6)

[9] *John Ford,* p. xvi.

Perhaps the finest tribute to Ford's characterization of Meleander, however, is that it is more than adequate to sustain interest in the fifth act, when, after the various lovers had been united, there was a grave danger that the play would simply collapse.

The second feature worthy of comment is the famous adaptation of the contest between the human singer and the nightingale. Ford's adaptation may lack the sheer virtuosity of Crashaw's but his technical skill shows in the way in which the meeting of bird and singer is adapted to dramatic instead of lyrical purposes; it is Menaphon's account of his first meeting with Parthenophill, and is skilfully broken up by the interested interjections of Amethus. It comes, too, at the right point of the play; we have just learnt of two pairs of lovers and need an introduction to the third heroine which will keep her clear in our minds. The famous 'contention' does achieve this.

Thirdly, the humour of the play must at least be mentioned. Ford has admitted in the prologue that he would wish it overlooked, and most readers have taken his advice or have severely criticized him for it. But the minor characters are not always dull in *The Lovers Melancholy*. Menaphon's opening conversation with Pelias has some amusing parody of the extravagance of courtly language (though we tire of this later) and it is not difficult to raise a smile at such exchanges as

*Rhetias.* Thou art no Scholler?
*Pelias.* I haue read Pamphlets dedicated to me.
(I. 293–4)

Cuculus (an early version of Bergetto in *'Tis Pitty*) and Grilla admittedly pall, and Trollio's attempts at humour do not succeed in setting off by contrast the tragedy of Meleander (if that was the intention). It is at boisterous and sustained verbal humour that Ford fails; one can only wish that he had had the courage of his convictions and had omitted the comic relief altogether.

Here again he was unfortunately bound by convention; and yet one wonders whether his innovations have been adequately appreciated. For if the main plot of *The Lovers Melancholy* were put in heroic couplets, the play could almost be by Dryden. In setting and in characterization it reminds one, for example, of

*Marriage à la Mode* and suggests again that there was no break in
the English dramatic tradition during the Commonwealth.
Dramatists like Ford as well as the writers of comedy were
clearly working in several different ways towards newer types
of drama; and although the last thing one would suggest is that
*The Lovers Melancholy* had a purely historical importance, it is
well to recognize that it was not a mere reworking of previous
plays.

It was Ford's first unaided drama and shows clearly some of
his limitations. The typical Elizabethan story of the girl in disguise is, as it were, put to the test of Burtonian psychology and
not found wanting. Precisely because the dramatist is inexperienced and anxious to leave no loose ends, he makes certain that
his characters are carefully balanced and his incidents neatly
contrived (much as the inexperienced student will try to achieve
form in an essay by writing on a purely chronological plan).
The result, of course, is a sense of contrivance rather than
inevitability; and, ironically, one remembers of *The Lovers
Melancholy* much what one remembers of the earlier plays
written in collaboration—single scenes and even single lines.
Ford did not work on the usual patterns of tragi-comedy; but
the play he wrote falls short of tragedy in much the same way
and is similarly remembered for its characters, its poetry and
its poetry of situation rather than as a dramatic whole.

# V

## The Broken Heart

*T*HE BROKEN HEART was entered on the Stationers' Register on 28 March 1633 and was published in that year, the title-page calling it 'A Tragedy' and noting that it had been 'Acted by the Kings Majesties Seruants at the priuate House in the Black-Friers'. It is, in part at least, another dramatic adaptation of types of Burtonian melancholy; like *The Lovers Melancholy* again, it seems to be conceived more or less as a series of set scenes; and it shares with that play its pervading tone of gravity and high seriousness.

The setting of *The Broken Heart* is, appropriately enough for a study of subdued passion, Sparta, albeit not so much the Sparta of history as that of Sidney's *Arcadia*. The Prologue, no less significant than Ford's prologues usually are, accordingly begins by mentioning this:

> OVr Scæne is *Sparta*. HE whose best of Art
> Hath drawne *this Peece*, cals it the *Broken Heart*.
> The Title lends no expectation here
> Of apish laughter, or of some lame Ieere
> At place or persons; no pretended clause
> Of iest's fit for a brothell Courts' applause
> From vulgar admiration: such low songs,
> Tun'd to vnchast eares, suit not modest tongues.
> The Virgine Sisters then deseru'd fresh bayes
> When *Innocence* and *Sweetnesse* crown'd their layes:
> Then vices gasp'd for breath, whose whole Commerce
> Was whip'd to Exile by vnblushing verse.
> This law we keepe in our Presentment now,
> Not to take freedome more then we allow;
> What may be here thought a *fiction*, when Times youth
> Wanted some riper yeares, was knowne *A Truth*:
> In which, if words haue cloath'd the subiect right,
> You may pertake, a Pitty, with Delight.

The most attractive theory of 'the truth' on which Ford claims to have based his play has been Sherman's[1] that Ford adapted the relationship of Sir Philip Sidney and Penelope Devereux.

---

[1]'Stella and *The Broken Heart*', *P.M.L.A.*, xxiv (1909), 275 ff.

Penthea's enforced marriage to Bassanes but refusal to yield to her confessed lover, Orgilus, does recall Penelope Devereux's marriage to Lord Rich against her will when promised to Sidney, and her subsequent refusal (apparently) to listen to her lover's pleas. (It is hardly relevant that the story of *Astrophel and Stella* may be purely conventional, for it is always possible that Ford may have taken it literally.) We do know, of course, from *Fames Memoriall* of Ford's interest in Lady Rich. There could, then, easily be some truth in Sherman's view; but one would need to add that Orgilus is hardly an adaptation of Astrophel, even in the broadest sense of the word 'adaptation'; the sterility of Penthea's husband, Bassanes, makes the situation of the play a special one; and the whole outcome of Ford's story is almost the opposite of Astrophel's resignation, in an inverted spirit of romance.

Ford's play is so well known that the story may be told very briefly. When it begins, Orgilus has been deprived of his promised bride, Penthea, who has been forced by her brother, Ithocles, remembering former enmity between the families, to marry Bassanes. This is told us in a rather slow and undramatic opening scene in which Orgilus gives these facts to his father, Crotolon, as his reason for wishing to go to Athens:

*Org.*                                           *Bassanes*
        The man that calls her wife; considers truly
        What Heaven of perfections he is Lord of,
        By thinking faire *Penthea* his: This thought
        Begets a kinde of Monster-Loue, which Loue
        Is nurse vnto a feare so strong, and seruile,
        As brands all dotage with a Iealousie.
        All eyes who gaze upon that shrine of beauty,
        He doth resolue, doe homage to the miracle;
        Some one, he is assur'd, may now or then
        (If opportunity but sort) preuaile:
        So much out of a selfe-vnworthinesse
        His feares transport him, not that he findes cause
        In her obedience, but his owne distrust.
*Crot.*  You spin out your discourse.
*Org.*                                  My griefs are violent;
        For knowing how the Maid was heretofore
        Courted by me, his iealousies grow wild
        That I should steale againe into her fauours,
        And vndermine her vertues: which the gods

Know I nor dare, nor dreame of: hence, from hence,
I vndertake a voluntary exile.
First, by my absence to take off the cares
Of Iealous *Bassanes*, but chiefly (Sir)
To free *Penthea* from a hell on earth:
Lastly, to lose the memory of something,
Her presence makes to liue in me afresh.

(i. 148–73)

It soon appears, however, that Orgilus is more interested in
revenge (the play has been called, not altogether aptly, 'a
revenge play without a villain'), particularly after he has once
again pleaded his cause in vain with Penthea. Eventually, after
Penthea's death, he murders Ithocles; and, condemned to death
by the Princess Calantha, chooses to die by letting his own blood.
Calantha, who had been in love with Ithocles, dies of a broken
heart.

The mere retelling of this story will perhaps suggest that there
are two main dangers in it for a Jacobean playwright—the
characters of Bassanes and Orgilus. Ford is not entirely successful with either.

Bassanes is another of the characters whom Ford based on
Burton. From Burton he takes his account of the symptoms of
the kind of jealousy promoted particularly by knowledge of one's
own sterility; and the portrait is not without a certain lifelike-
ness. Bassanes is given affection, of a kind, for Penthea, although
it is akin rather to pride in her than to feeling with her:

Shee comes, she comes, so shoots the morning forth,
Spangled with pearles of transparent dew . . .
We will to Court, where, if it be thy pleasure,
Thou shalt appeare in such a rauishing lustre
Of Iewels aboue value, that the Dames
Who braue it there, in rage to be out-shin'd,
Shall hide them in their Closets, and unseene
Fret in their teares; whiles euery wondring eye
Shall craue none other brightnesse but thy presence.
Choose thine owne recreations, be a Queene
Of what delights thou fanciest best, what company,
What place, what times, doe any thing, doe all things
Youth can command; so thou wilt chase these clouds
From the pure firmament of thy faire lookes.

(ii. 633–4, 642–53)

He also comes to life with his bitter asides and generalizations

from his own theoretical experience, when he makes his contribution to the congratulating of Prophilus and Euphranea on
their betrothal:

> The ioyes of marriage are the heauen on earth,
> Life's paradise (great Princesse) the soules quiet,
> Sinewes of concord, earthly immortality,
> Eternity of pleasures; no restoratiues
> Like to a constant woman.—(but where is she?
> 'Twould puzzle all the gods, but to create
> Such a new monster.)—I can speake by proofe,
> For I rest in *Elizium*, 'tis my happinesse.
>
> (II. 819–826)

But already in his opening speech a little earlier he has been
reduced almost to the level of farce by his plans to keep Penthea
from temptation:

> I'le haue that window next the street dam'd vp;
> It giues too full a prospect to temptation,
> And courts a Gazers glances: there's a lust
> Committed by the eye, that sweats, and trauels,
> Plots, wakes, contriues, till the deformed bear-whelpe
> Adultery be lick'd into the act,
> The very act; that light shall be dam'd vp
>
> (II. 564–70)

and he is hardly credible when he bursts in on Penthea and her
brother Ithocles, accusing them of 'bestiall incest'. One can see
what is happening here. Ford is trying to draw a man whose
jealousy does bring him to the very verge of insanity; and no
doubt seventeenth-century theory demanded that his jealousy
should appear absurd before he would recognize it for what it
was (I am thinking here of Jonson bringing men out of their
humours at least as much as of Burton). In the later part of the
play, after the death of Penthea, Bassanes is a credible and even
likeable figure, with his new-found stoicism and dignity, fittingly
recognized by Calantha in her testamentary arrangements for
the welfare of Sparta. But, agreeing whole-heartedly with Dr
Tillyard when he says[2] 'that the Elizabethans constructed their
characters on rigid academic, *a priori* suppositions does not mean
that they were incapable of first-hand observation', one can
still say of Bassanes that he is drawn from Burton rather than

[2]*Shakespeare's History Plays* (London, 1944), pp. 280–1.

life—and perhaps that this is typical of the ways in which *The Broken Heart* falls short of *'Tis Pitty* and seems to be a less mature play.

Orgilus, the other crucial character, has motive enough for all his actions, in the loss of Penthea because of her brother's impetuous vindictiveness. But like most of the Elizabethan and Jacobean revengers, Orgilus suffers from a certain staginess. Ford seems to picture him as a personable and plausible young man, one who can be firm or pliant as the situation demands and who can proceed always with one end in view. But his methods of arriving at that end do not always hold our full interest.

For example, his desire to conceal his identity from Prophilus and Euphranea, when he is disguised as a student, is understandable enough. But when Ford makes him rant in this way he is merely being conventional:

> I am discovered—Say it: is it possible
> With a smooth tongue, a leering countenance,
> Flattery, or force of reason (—I come t'ee Sir)
> To turne, or to appease the raging Sea?
> Answer to that,—your Art? what Art to catch
> And hold fast in a net the Sunnes small Atomes?
> No, no; they'll out, they'll out; ye may as easily
> Out run a Cloud, driuen by a Northerne blast,
> As fiddle faddle so. Peace, or speake sense.
>
> (I. 480–8)

Similarly, Orgilus's demand that his sister Euphranea should not marry without his consent gives opportunities for effective single scenes but does not come to anything in the long run. Euphranea wishes to marry Prophilus, the friend of Ithocles; and Ford achieves some effective irony when Orgilus (in disguise) comments on a conversation he overhears:

*Proph.* Bright *Euphranea*,
Should I repeat old vowes, or study new,
For purchase of beleefe to my desires—
*Org.* Desires?
*Proph.* My seruice, my integrity—
*Org.* That's better.
*Proph.* I should but repeat a lesson
Oft conn'd without a prompter; but thine eyes,
My Loue is honourable—
*Org.* So was mine
To my *Penthea*: chastly honourable . . . (I. 430–7)

Bitter irony as a dramatic device appeals to Ford as much as to
Webster; it occurs again in the scene in which Orgilus pretends
friendship to Ithocles:

| | |
|---|---|
| *Org.* | O my good Lord, your fauours flow towards |
| | A too vnworthy worme; but as you please, |
| | I am what you will shape me. |
| *Itho.* | A fast friend. |
| *Crot.* | I thanke thee sonne for this acknowledgement, |
| | It is a sight of gladnesse. |
| *Org.* | But my duty. |

(III. 1515–19)

It is found yet again when Orgilus with his tongue in his cheek
sings the praises of Ithocles to Calantha's suitor the Prince of
Argos, hoping to incense Ithocles further by the irony which he
alone understands:

> For *Ithocles* in fashion of his mind
> Is beautifull, soft, gentle, the cleare mirror
> Of absolute perfection
>
> (IV. 1722–4).

There is telling irony also (although this time apparent only to
the audience) when Orgilus quietly agrees with Armostes that

> Griefes will haue their vent.
>
> (IV. 1759)

But for all this, sympathy with Orgilus is mainly in the scenes
in which he appears with Penthea. There he is a tragic figure,
as he pleads his love:

> I would possesse my wife, the equity
> Of very reason bids me.
>
> (II. 947–8)

Penthea tells us:

> Alas poore Gentleman,
> 'A look'd not like the ruines of his youth,
> But like the ruines of those ruines
>
> (II. 1004–6)

And he is still both an heroic and a pathetic figure as he watches
Penthea as her reason fails and realizes he can do nothing to
help her:

> some angry Minister of Fate hath
> Depos'd the Empresse of her soule, her reason,
> From its most proper Throne; but what's the miracle
> More new, I, I haue seene it, and yet liue.
>
> (IV. 1852–5)

Interest in Orgilus, however, tends to pass with Penthea: and it is difficult for the modern reader, at any rate, to continue to believe in him as he catches Ithocles in his 'engine' (a folding chair that holds the victim fast while he is murdered). That scene is both melodramatic and conventional, and Orgilus hardly recovers our full interest even in his chosen Spartan death and final words (with their noticeable echo of Webster's Flamineo):

*Bass.* Life's fountaine is dry'd vp.
*Org.* So falls the Standards
Of my prerogatiue in being a creature:
A mist hangs o're mine eyes; the Sun's bright splendor
Is clouded in an euerlasting shadow:
Welcome thou yce that sit'st about my heart,
No heat can euer thaw thee. (v. 2499–504)

With Orgilus, Ford seems still to be leaning heavily on previous drama, from which he takes ideas of what people might say in given situations; the result is good, but it is not pure Ford. One does question, however, whether any other playwright could have drawn Penthea; in her is the full strength of the play.

Sherman has suggested that 'In *The Broken Heart* Ford throws down the gauntlet to orthodox morality by placing a thoroughly pure woman in a genuine moral dilemma'.[3] I do not think Penthea's situation is as unprecedented in drama as that statement would suggest; and I know of no evidence that Ford had an axe to grind. But he did, clearly, see the dramatic (as against the purely ethical) possibilities in the conflict that Sherman has described.

Penthea is torn between two rights, which she regards as two wrongs: Orgilus has a claim on her as the man she loves, Bassanes has one as her husband, and so Penthea is distraught:

There is no peace left for a rauish'd wife
Widdow'd by lawlesse marriage (IV. 1953–4)

Sensabaugh, thinking of her description of herself to Ithocles as

a faith-breaker,
A spotted whore, forgiue me; I am one
In art, not in desires, the gods must witnesse . . .
For she that's wife to *Orgilus*, and liues
In knowne Adultery with *Bassanes*,
Is at the best a whore (III. 1196–8, 1200–02),

[3] *'Tis Pitty'* and *'The Broken Heart'*, p. xxvii.

writes that 'Penthea cries to the world that her name has been strumpeted simply because in a physical sense she stayed true to her husband, Bassanes'. (pp. 180–1) The point is surely rather that she regards herself as a strumpet because she allowed herself to be married to Bassanes when she loved Orgilus and so virtually sold her body to one she did not care for:

> cruelty enforc'd
> Diuorce betwixt my body and my heart.
>
> (II. 932–3)

Unless 'orthodox morality' argues that enforced marriage to a man one hates must alter even one's feelings to the man one loves, it is hard to see what wrong there is in that, for never does Penthea think of breaking her marriage vows, however Orgilus may stress his lover's 'rights'. She even sincerely advises him to marry another, asking only that he think of her 'with mercy, not contempt' and hoping that his wife will not scorn her fall. The more one examines Ford's allegedly daring assaults on conventional morality, the more absurd the charge becomes.

Penthea's first word is 'alas' and it is clear that the dramatist's problem was to present her in her grief as always a pathetic figure and yet not sentimentalize her. I believe he succeeds brilliantly in the task, and he succeeds partly because he refuses to make Penthea completely weak. She is no Desdemona, willing to forgive all, but a woman of spirit, quite able to make certain that Ithocles realizes the enormity of his action before she forgives him for it; and she never loses her dignity even with the impossible Bassanes.

One of Ford's finest scenes is that now usually numbered II. iii., when Penthea meets Orgilus by accident in the garden. He throws off his disguise, claiming her pity for his situation. Pity is given, but Penthea follows it with some of the most memorable lines in Ford, lines in which his favourite trick of repetition and the 'falling cadence' suggest perfectly Penthea's grief, love and determination:

> Haue you ought else to vrge
> Of new demand? as for the old forget it,
> 'Tis buried in an everlasting silence,
> And shall be, shall be euer; what more would ye?
>
> (II. 943–6)

Orgilus's further claims on her meet with indignant and even
passionate rebuttal, and it is only after he has gone that her true
feeling for him comes out undisguised:

> 'A sigh'd my name sure as he parted from me,
> I feare I was too rough.
>
> (II. 1003–4)

The same plaintive note is sustained through the later scene in
which Penthea asks Calantha to look favourably on the suit of
Ithocles.

> *Calan.*　　　You haue forgot, *Penthea*,
> How still I haue a father.
> *Pen.*　　　　　　But remember
> I am a sister, though to me this brother
> Hath beene you know vnkinde: ô most vnkinde
>
> (III. 1624–7)

Even the scenes in which Penthea's reason begins to go are
not allowed to sink into bathos. Interestingly, the spotlight is
kept, as it were, rather on those around her, in their distress,
than on Penthea herself; but she is given some moving lines—
lines which are all the more moving because the Penthea of the
earlier scenes would not have asked for sympathy in this way:

> Since I was first a wife, I might haue beene
> Mother to many pretty pratling Babes:
> They would haue smil'd when I smil'd; and, for certaine,
> I should haue cry'd when they cry'd;—truly brother,
> My father would haue pick'd me out a husband,
> And then my little ones had beene no bastards:
> But 'tis too late for me to marry now,
> I am past child-bearing; 'tis not my fault.
>
> (IV. 1894–1901)

The same pathetic contrast with the past is suggested by the
lines

> 　　　　　　　Remember
> When we last gather'd Roses in the garden
> I found my wits, but truly you lost yours
>
> (IV. 1926–8)

Mr T. S. Eliot has rightly been taken to task for his too ready
assumption that these lines are 'quite irrelevant and apparently
meaningless'.[4] The excuse is that in the original Quarto they

[4]*Elizabethan Essays*, p. 143.

are given to Orgilus; but the knowledge of Ithocles's love for
Calantha shown both in the preceding lines and in the following
line of the same speech, and also Ithocles's comment

> Poore soule, how idely
> Her fancies guide her tongue
>
> (IV. 1929–30)

prove that they belong to Penthea. Her mind wanders back,
Marguerite-like, to the scene in the garden when Orgilus
claimed her as his own and she rejected him; in comparison
with her present state, that was happiness; and she, who knows
that she is now wandering in her mind, knows also that she was
certainly the sane one then. The lines, then, so far from being
irrelevant and meaningless, add the final touch of pathos to a
most moving portrayal.

Ithocles is also well drawn; his tragedy comes from his recognition both of his earlier sin when he acted in youthful haste and
of his inability, although he is a man of action, to do anything to
rectify it. He can only utter, humbly but with dignity, his
regret:

> No reprehensions Vncle, I deserue 'em.
> Yet gentle Sir, consider what the heat
> Of an vnsteady youth, a giddy braine,
> Greene indiscretion, flattery of greatnesse,
> Rawnesse of iudgement, wilfulnesse in folly,
> Thoughts vagrant as the wind, and as vncertaine,
> Might lead a boy in yeeres too; 'twas a fault,
> A Capitall fault, for then I could not diue
> Into the secrets of commanding Loue:
> Since when, experience by the extremities (in others)
> Hath forc'd me to collect. And trust me *Crotolon*,
> I will redeeme those wrongs with any seruice
> Your satisfaction can require for currant.
>
> (II. 774–86)

The next part of his punishment comes when he conceives his
love for the Princess Calantha to be just as incapable of fruition
as that of Orgilus for Penthea. His happiness in his discovery
that the love is reciprocated is but brief; it is, of course, cut short
by Orgilus.

I cannot but feel it a slight weakness in the play that at the
end we are asked to concentrate not on any of these four but on
Calantha. In the early acts she is well presented as the very type

of a princess, proud, stately, saying always the right thing at the
right time, whether it be to her unwelcome suitor the Prince of
Argos, to Ithocles or merely to Orgilus, but having a mind of
her own and capable of getting her own way, as when she sees
to it that it is Ithocles and not the Prince whose arm she accepts
(III. 1417–19) and that it is Ithocles who takes up the ring that
the Prince has asked for. Nor does she forget to be a Princess
when Penthea comes to tell her of the love of Ithocles:

> What new change
> Appeares in my behauiour, that thou dar'st
> Tempt my displeasure?
>
> (III. 1614–16).

Penthea has to be content with the cryptic

> Lady,
> Your checke lyes in my silence.
>
> (II. 1628–9)

There is, then, no inconsistency in the behaviour of Calantha
when, as she is dancing at the nuptials of Prophilus and
Euphranea, news is brought to her, in rapid succession, of the
deaths of her father, of Penthea and of Ithocles, and she dances
on. But there is no point in it, no motive beyond the Spartan
desire to conceal feelings. And that motive would hardly seem
to apply to her 'coronation' and her 'marriage' to the dead
Ithocles, so that her explanation, except for its famous penul-
timate[5] line, falls flat:

> ô my Lords,
> I but deceiu'd your eyes with Anticke gesture,
> When one newes straight came hudling on another,
> Of death, and death, and death, still I danc'd forward,
> But it strooke home, and here, and in an instant,
> Be such meere women, who with shreeks and out-cries
> Can vow a present end to all their sorrowes,
> Yet liue to vow new pleasures, and out-liue them:
> They are the silent griefes which cut the hart-strings;
> Let me dye smiling.
>
> (v. 2586–95)

[5]Sensabaugh (p. 34) points to Burton's '*And hard is the choice* (as it is in *Euphues*)
*when one is compelled either by silence to dye with griefe, or by speaking to liue with shame*'
as the probable source of Ford's famous line. But the thought is a commonplace,
deriving perhaps originally from Seneca; and it is found in Shakespeare and
Webster.

Her death of a broken heart comes as something of an anti-climax.

The truth about the famous ending, praised so highly by Lamb and by many since, would seem to be that it is the result of Ford's desire for a sensational climax and that it is there for its own sake, as the best scenes in Ford are not. It is typical of the breaking-up of late Jacobean drama into individual scenes. It is also given a certain artificiality by its being something like a postscript; and that is so because *The Broken Heart* like *The Lovers Melancholy* has more than one set of main characters and has to turn from one to the other at the end.

I think it wrong to imply that Ford could not do better. Even in the use of the minor characters like Lemophil,[6] Christalla, Groneas and Philema, whose trivial loves are apparently intended to throw into greater relief the seriousness of the main plot, one has what is rather a tentative approach to a dramatic technique than its culmination.

*The Broken Heart*, in its careful psychological exposition, of Penthea and of Orgilus particularly, is fine enough to win fame for any dramatist; but if others of Ford's plays have perhaps numerically more weaknesses, if one chooses to count them, I believe they also have less of that air of melodrama that is felt throughout *The Broken Heart*. The play, I suggest, has to '*Tis Pitty* much the same relation as Webster's *Duchess of Malfi* has to *The White Devil*. Of *The Broken Heart* as of *The Duchess of Malfi* it is fatally easy to say that it is quieter, more restrained, more poetic than the play with which it is being compared; one should surely add that it is also less credible and in both subject and treatment essentially less dramatic.

[6]The character is called Lemophil in the list of 'Speakers names, fitted to their Qualities' and at least once in the text, but appears elsewhere as Hemophil. Most of Ford's editors have preferred the second form, but surely in error, in view of Ford's gloss of the name as 'Glutton'.

# VI

## *The Queen* and *Loves Sacrifice*

IT NEED not surprise if the next two plays do not reach the standard of *The Lovers Melancholy* and *The Broken Heart*. These had their limitations but marked a very high level of achievement; and in turning from them to plays of a different kind, the dramatist was bound at first to make new errors. *The Queen* and *Loves Sacrifice* may still be compared to the temporary loss of ground which means ultimate advance.

*The Queen, or the Excellency of her Sex* is an anonymous work, published in 1653 as 'An Excellent old Play. Found out by a Person of Honour, and given to the Publisher, Alexander Goughe'. Goughe was a former actor with the King's Men and is, for example, listed as a player in *The Lovers Melancholy*, in which he probably took a woman's part.

The play was confidently attributed to Ford by Professor Bang when he edited it as volume xiii of his *Materialien zur Kunde des älteren Englischen Dramas*. A few of his parallel passages count for nothing, since some of the phrasing involved is conventional, but the evidence as a whole is overwhelming. S. P. Sherman,[1] Dugdale Sykes[2] and Miss Sargeaunt have each added to the evidence; and the signs of Ford's hand are so frequent and so evenly distributed throughout the play that it seems impossible that any other playwright could have had even a collaborator's part in it.

It is equally clear that *The Queen* adds nothing to Ford's dramatic reputation. It may well have been because of a conviction that the play did not count for much that he did not publish it himself. I should also like to suggest that he might have regarded *Loves Sacrifice* as a better attempt at the same kind of story, each of the plays treating a husband's baseless suspicion of the chastity of his wife.

The plot of *The Queen* is all but ridiculous in execution. In conception it was possibly not so: Bang interestingly quotes in this connection Calantha's words from *The Broken Heart*:

[1] 'A New Play by Ford', *Modern Language Notes*, xxiii (1909), 245–9.
[2] *Sidelights*, ch. viii.

71

> A woman has enough to gouerne wisely
> Her owne demeanours, passions, and diuisions.
> A Nation warlike and inur'd to practice
> Of policy and labour, cannot brooke
> A feminate authority: we therefore
> Command your counsaile, how you may aduise vs
> In choosing of a husband whose abilities
> Can better guide this kingdome.
>
> (v. 2527–34)

and comments 'Es sieht so aus, als wären diese Verse ein An-
zeichen dafür, dass Forde mit dem Gedanken *The Queene* zu
dichten umging, als er die letzte Hand an *The Broken Heart*
legte'. (p. 46) For this is the opening situation of *The Queen*.

Alphonso, who hates all womankind (the dramatist begins
with this as an hypothesis, in the true style of tragi-comedy) has
led a revolt against the Queen of Arragon and has been condemned to death. But at the last minute the Queen reprieves
him and marries him. After the marriage, he asks that they may
live apart for a week, so that he may

> redeem a while some serious thoughts
> Which have misdeem'd your sex.
>
> (I. 675-6)

But the week grows into a month; and the division becomes
worse when Muretto deliberately arouses Alphonso's suspicions
of his wife's chastity, suggesting that she has been unfaithful
with Petruchi. The poison has already begun to work when we
first hear of this, so that again an improbable situation has to be
taken on trust; but the scenes in which Muretto actually incites
Alphonso are better and are reminiscent, as are the similar
D'avolos scenes in *Loves Sacrifice*, of *Othello*; and in both plays
Ford uses the interesting alternation of prose for the tempter and
verse for the anger and agony of the husband. Alphonso, whose
jealousy is again apparently based on the Burtonian formula,
as Sensabaugh has pointed out, decrees that the Queen must
die unless a champion appears to defend her; and the Queen
forbids any of her adherents to be so false to her as to appear
against her husband.

Side by side with this plot is developing the story of the widow
Salassa, who commands the Queen's general Velasco, as proof
of his love for her (it is another incredible infatuation) to behave

in public as if he were a coward. Then she pawns her life to say
that he will appear as the Queen's champion; he refuses, until
she is on the very scaffold; and then all ends well, improbably
enough, for Alphonso sees reason when he finds that the Queen
has as champions not only Velasco and Petruchi but also
Muretto, who announces that his insinuations have all been
conscious attempts to arouse Alphonso's jealousy and so make
him appreciate his Queen (Muretto interestingly combines the
functions of the physician Corax in *The Lovers Melancholy* and
the tempter D'avolos in *Loves Sacrifice*).

It has not, I think, been pointed out that the relationship of
the two plots is not confined to Velasco's appearances in the
early and the final scenes. Ford seems to have intended that
each should be a study of 'policy'. Alphonso sees himself, somewhat suddenly, it must be confessed, as a skilful 'politician':

> So, so, far reaching pollicy, I adore thee . . .
> Henceforth my Stratagem's of scorn and hatred
> Shall kill in smiles. I will not strike and frown,
> But laugh and murther.
>
> (II. 1590, 1596–1600)

and Salassa is described by Lodovico:

> Well, lady, you are as pestilent a piece of policy,
> as ever made an ass of love.
>
> (IV. 2689–91)

Moreover, Salassa begins to love Velasco, as Alphonso begins
to love the Queen, when circumstances arising from that
'policy' seem to make the union impossible. The further intention could even have been that the pointlessness of Salassa's
'policy' should throw into relief the tragedy of Alphonso's; but,
of course, the handling of the story of Alphonso is not skilful
enough for this to be the result. Nevertheless, this use of a minor
plot to echo and yet contrast with the major marks a further
stage in Ford's development. In *The Queen* he still has two sets of
figures in the serious plots, as opposed to the comic; but the story
of one of these sets, Salassa and Velasco, has been subordinated
to the story of the other, the Queen and Alphonso, whereas no
pair of lovers in *The Lovers Melancholy* is subordinate to any
other, and the Orgilus-Penthea, Ithocles-Calantha tragedies in
*The Broken Heart* are of equal importance. It is not until the next

play, *Loves Sacrifice*, that Ford takes the further step towards simplicity of design, of concentrating almost entirely on one major group of figures—husband, wife and lover.

Characterization in *The Queen* perhaps pays the price for Ford's experimenting. For the most part, Alphonso is a stagy figure. The motivation is all so inadequate that one begins to wonder (and the doubt increases as Ford progresses) whether Ford was really interested in plot at all.[3] In *The Queen*, at any rate, one has no sympathy with a man who has created a difficulty and then begins to pity himself for it. But if one *can* forget the occasion, one can appreciate the exposition of the emotion, particularly as Ford seems to be deliberately portraying the grief of one who is a sentimentalist at heart. Muretto makes the point when he tells Alphonso

> Besides, women (my lord) are all creatures, not
> Gods nor Angels
>
> (IV. 2466–7)

But when Alphonso is not hating, he is romanticizing:

> I have surveyed the wonder of her cheeks,
> Compar'd them with the lillies and the rose
> And by my life, *Muretto*, Roses are
> Adulterate to her blush, and lilies pale,
> Examin'd with her white; yet, blear eyed fool,
> I could not see those rarities before me.
>
> (IV. 2407–15)

and not even Muretto's treatment can cure him of that:

> Let's kneel to this (what shall I call her?) Woman?
> No, she's an Angel. Glory of Creation,
> Can you forget my wickedness?
>
> (V. 3642–6)

It must be admitted, however, that only a sophisticated audience could appreciate such finer shades of characterization; and only an unsophisticated one could willingly endure the premises from which the dramatist starts. That, in brief, is the problem of all Jacobean tragi-comedy.

The Queen herself is not a completely sympathetic character: she is too weak and her anger against those who criticize

---

[3] I think the paradox is justified. Motivation links the character of one scene with the same character in another—a matter of continuity, as against the analysis of a single emotion.

Alphonso is so unwarranted that it merely irritates us. Muretto
is hardly consistent, Salassa and Velasco are there for the plot
rather than for themselves, and the really minor figures, like
Bufo and Pynto, are nearly always dull, although Ford does
occasionally raise a smile here, as in Mopas's ironical support of
Bufo's attempt to steel himself to fight:

though your throat be cut in your own defence, 'tis but manslaughter,
you can never be hang'd for it.

(IV. 3004–6)

Perhaps, too, he began with Bufo, Pynto and Muretto in an
attempt, praiseworthy though unsuccessful, to improve on the
obvious exposition of the opening scenes of *The Lovers Melancholy*
and *The Broken Heart*.

The prose of the subplot has a certain ease that is not found
in the prose of Ford's dedications, and the verse at its best is
fluent and has a rhetorical power that was not the least of Ford's
merits as a poet. This is seen, for example, in the working up to
its quite unexpected conclusion of Alphonso's speech from the
scaffold:

Tender, Madam,
I kiss your Royal hand, and call you fair,
Assure this noble, this uncovered presence,
That richest vertue is your bosoms tenant,
That you are absolutely great and good;
I'll flatter all the vices of your sex,
Protesting men are monsters, women Angels,
No light ones, but full weighty, natures best,
I'll proclaim lust a pitty, pride a handsomness.
Deceit ripness of wit, bold scandalous scolding,
A bravery of spirit; bloody cruelty,
Masculine justice; more I will maintain
That Queens are chief for rule, you chief of Queens,
If you'l but give me leave to die in peace.
Pray give me leave to die.

(I. 401–25)

The other feature of the play to which I would draw attention is the deliberate echoing of Shakespeare, not only in the
main *Othello*-like situation but also in odd phrasing here and
there, such as Bufo's 'But i'thy face, I'll have no buts' (I. 184),
the Queen's 'Wherein my gratious Lord have I offended?' (II.
1132) and Pynto's appeal 'my lord the King; My Jove, justice,

justice' (v. 3757–8). The first of these may be accidental; but
was the second perhaps intended to bring with it some of the
dignity of Katherine's appeal to Henry VIII? And does not the
third imply that Pynto flatters himself by seeing himself as a
wronged Falstaff?

Nor, indeed, is this echoing confined to Shakespeare. Pynto's
'Come from that slippery Ele, Captain' (I. 46–7) suggests immediately to me Cyril Tourneur's 'Come from that poysonous
woman there' and one wonders whether it was intended to
suggest it to Ford's audience. Apparently it is part of the folly of
these pretentious fools to quote and misquote previous drama.
(There are other examples.)

At the very least it can be said that *The Queen* is interesting
because of the development in it of many of his characteristic
mannerisms and methods of working.

*Loves Sacrifice*, I have suggested, deals with a similar theme. In
it Ford seems to have set himself the problem of steering between
the *Othello* situation, used in *The Queen*, of a husband's wrongful
suspicions of a faithful wife, and the common dramatic subject
of the husband's revenge on an unfaithful one. He seems to have
asked himself what would happen if the wife did not actually
commit adultery but did openly show her love for another man;
and thereby *Loves Sacrifice* is linked also to *The Broken Heart* in
that each deals with a woman 'widdow'd' by marriage to the
wrong man (I believe that this is what Crashaw's allegedly
enigmatic couplet means). The result is not altogether happy,
although the play seems to have had a certain success; it was
entered on the Stationers' Register and published in 1633 and
remained in the repertory until at least 1639, when it was one
of a long list of plays, including '*Tis Pitty* and *The Spanish Gipsie*,
protected by the Lord Chamberlain against acting by other
companies, on behalf of Beeston's Boys (The King and Queen's
Young Company).[4]

It is the story of the impetuous, volatile Duke of Pavy who
prides himself on having, in his newly-wedded wife Biancha and
his friend Fernando, 'a perfect Friend, a Wife aboue compare'
(I. 219). He bids his wife hold Fernando dear, in words that are

[4]Bentley, i. 330–1.

seen to be pregnant with dramatic irony in exactly the style of
the opening of *The Witch of Edmonton*:

> Looke, *Biancha*,
> On this good man; in all respects to him
> Be as to me: onely the name of husband,
> And reuerent obseruance of our bed
> Shall differ vs in persons, else in soule
> We are all one.

*Bian.* I shall, in best of Loue,
> Regard the bosome-partner of my Lord.    (i. 229–36)

Fernando falls in love with Biancha and tells her of it. She
twice rejects him haughtily, although the dramatist perhaps
intends to suggest, by her *twice-used* threat that if ever Fernando
speaks so again she will reveal all to the Duke, that it is already
Fernando she loves and not her husband. Nevertheless it is somewhat of a shock to the reader when Biancha comes to Fernando
at night and says he may have his will of her, but that if she
yields and thereby breaks her marriage vows, she will kill herself afterwards. Fernando feels that he must accept the position;
they swear to remain chaste.

*Fer.* I must beleeue ye, yet I hope anon,
> When you are parted from me, you will say
> I was a good cold easie-spirited man:
> Nay, laugh at my simplicity; say, will ye?

*Bian.* No by the faith I owe my Bridall vowes:
> But euer hold thee much much dearer farre
> Then all my ioyes on earth, by this chast kisse.

*Fer.* You haue preuail'd, and heauen forbid that I
> Should by a wanton appetite prophane
> This sacred Temple; 'tis enough for me
> You'll please to call me seruant.

*Bian.* Nay, be thine:
> Command my power, my bosome; and I'le write
> This loue within the tables of my heart.

*Fer.* Enough; I'le master passion, and triumph
> In being conquer'd; adding to it this,
> In you my loue, as it begun, shall end.

*Bian.* The latter I new vow—but day comes on,
> What now we leaue vnfinish'd of content,
> Each houre shall perfect vp: Sweet, let's part.

*Fer.* This kisse,—best life good rest.

*Bian.* All mine to thee.

> Remember this, and thinke I speake thy words:
> *When I am dead, rip vp my heart and read*
> *With constant eyes, what now my tongue defines,*
> *Fernando's name caru'd out in bloody lines.*
> Once more good rest, Sweet.
>
> *Fer.*    Your most faithfull seruant.

(II. 1358-85)

It will be clear that while some of the lines ring true, the scene as a whole does not convince.

The Duke's suspicions are aroused by his sister Fiormonda (a widow, who in the true style of tragi-comedy lusts after Fernando) and his secretary D'avolos. He is made to find Biancha and Fernando together; and he murders her—not, he says, because she loved another but because he believes she actually committed adultery:

> Faire diuell, in thy prayers reckon vp
> The summe, in grosse, of all thy vayned follies:
> There, amongst other, weepe in teares of blood,
> For one aboue the rest; *Adultery*,
> *Adultery*, *Biancha*; such a guilt,
> As were the sluces of thine eyes let vp,
> Teares cannot wash it off: 'tis not the tyde
> Of triuiall wontonnesse from youth to youth,
> But thy abusing of thy lawfull bed,
> Thy husbands bed; his, in whose brest thou sleep'st:
> His, that did prize thee more then all the trash
> Which hoarding worldlings make an Idoll of:
> When thou shalt find the Catalogue enrold
> Of thy mis-deeds, there shall be writ, in Text,
> Thy bastarding, the issues of a Prince.

(V. 2507-21)

Actual adultery, of course, is the sin which Biancha did not commit; and Fernando is spared once he convinces the Duke that Biancha did in fact remain chaste.

The Duke (and I do suggest again that Ford is setting out, as in *The Queen*, to present an abnormal nature, one that easily runs to extremes) goes to pay his respects at Biancha's tomb. In his new state of mind, he sees himself as

> That Butcher, who in my enraged spleene
> Slaughtered the *life of Innocence and Beauty*

(V. 2753-4)

one whose 'impious hand' will only

                    prophane the shrine
          Of fairest purity, which houers yet
          About those blessed bones inhearst within
                    (v. 2743-5).

From the tomb, Fernando appears in his winding sheet,
demanding that the Duke 'Forbeare'. When the guards go to
lay hands on him, he drinks a vial of poison and dies. The Duke,
seeing Fernando again now, somewhat surprisingly, as 'a friend
vnmatch'd', stabs himself; and Fiormonda and D'avolos receive
their punishment at the hands of his successor.

   Perhaps it is to be expected that descriptions of such a play
should differ. Hartley Coleridge, in his edition, says that *Loves
Sacrifice* is a 'most unsavoury offering . . . and contains little to
atone for a disgusting story, clumsily plotted, and characters
essentially vile';[5] and Swinburne finds it 'utterly indecent, un-
seemly and unfit for handling'.[6] Sherman calls it 'a problem
play' and takes the praise of Biancha and Fernando at the end,
for remaining physically chaste, as an attack on conventional
morality;[7] and Parrott and Ball echo him with '*Love's Sacrifice*
is not a revenge tragedy. It might more fitly be called a problem
play and the problem springs from the Astrophel-Stella story'—
that is, supposing the husband to have objected to Astrophel's
courting of Stella.[8] All these views seem to me somewhat far-
fetched.

   In the first place, no actual problem is stated by the dramatist.
In the play, no guilty party—on the strictest theory of morality
—escapes death; even in the subplot, Ferentes, the philanderer,
is killed by the women he has wronged; and whatever the Duke
may say about Biancha and Fernando at the end when he
blames himself for their deaths, the dramatist himself cannot be
said to condone their behaviour. Whatever the position might
have been in a comedy or tragi-comedy where Biancha and
Fernando had been let live, there can be no question in Ford's
tragedy of an argument for free love.

   Secondly, as against Parrott and Ball, it may be suggested
that instead of Sidney (or even Burton, who again provides the

[5] *The Dramatic Works of Massinger and Ford* (London, 1840), p. lviii.
[6] *Works*, xii. 381.
[7] Bang, *Materialien*, xxiii, Introductory Essay.
[8] *A Short View of Elizabethan Drama*, p. 244.

symptoms of the Duke's and Fernando's love-melancholy)[9] the
main source is again previous drama and particularly
Shakespeare. *Loves Sacrifice* should be seen as a reworking of the
*Othello* theme; and the correspondence is not confined to the
main D'avolos—Duke—Biancha: Iago—Othello—Desdemona
relationship but extends even to minor details. For example, the
untimely pleading by Biancha and Fernando for the restoration
to favour of Roseilli (and later of Maurucio) is a variation on
the Desdemona—Cassio story; and D'avolos's methods of
arousing the Duke are exactly Iago's. I need only quote, noting
even the Duke's exclamation:

*R.D.* (D'avolos)  Beshrew my heart, but that's not so good.
*Duke*         Ha, what's that thou mislik'st *D'auolos?*
*R.D.*         Nothing, my Lord
                                      (III. 1608–10)
or
*R.D.*  A shrewd ominous token; I like not that neither.
*Duke*  Againe! what is't you like not?
*R.D.*  I beseech your Highnesse excuse me
                                      (III. 1626–8)
or
*R.D.*  Bitter girds if all were knowne,—but—
*Duke*  But what? speake out; plague on your muttering
        Grumbling, I heare you, Sir, what is't?
*R.D.*  Nothing, I protest, to your Highnesse pertinent, to
        any moment.
                                      (III. 1680–4)

The hints rankle in the Duke's mind exactly as in Othello's;
and D'avolos's cunning even takes the Iago-like form of begging
his victim not to be too rash in his reasoning and his actions.

I believe I need not pursue that further; but I might add that
there are echoes also of *Romeo and Juliet* (the dying speeches of
Ferentes, III. 1856–61 and 1889–95, are clearly modelled on
Mercutio's, and the final scene in the tomb when Fernando
drinks the poison hardly needs his 'I come Biancha' to recall
Romeo). Ford also obviously had *The White Devil* in his mind
when he began his play with Roseilli's 'Depart the court' as
Webster began with Lodovico's 'Banished!', and used the same
character to tidy up at the end. (Here again he is striving for the

[9]See Sensabaugh, op. cit. and 'Ford's Tragedy of Love-Melancholy', *Englische Studien*, lxxiii (1939), 212–19.

impressive beginning; but Roseilli's words, though ominous, do not introduce the main theme of the play and are even misleading. The main exposition duly follows and is not dramatic at all.)

Thirdly, one might rephrase such of the objections to *Loves Sacrifice* as are based on the crudity of the subplot and say that it is not disgusting so much as dull. Parrott and Ball are the only critics, apparently, who have had sufficient patience with it to see that it was 'probably meant to contrast with the idealized passion of the hero' (although they still regard it as 'offensive'). Not only, I think, is the wanton Ferentes a foil to Fernando but also the story of Ferentes's philandering with Julia, Colona and Morona is intended to provide the 'Italian' atmosphere for the play, as the quarrelling retainers provide it in *Romeo and Juliet*:

> he that is not a Cuckold, or a Bastard,
> Is a strangely happy man; for a chaste wife, or a mother
> That neuer stept awry, are wonders, wonders in *Italy*.
>
> (I. 394–6)

In this, *Loves Sacrifice* marks another distinct advance on *The Queen*. But admittedly, when one has said that the subplot has this function and that it does provide an occasional smile in the clown Maurucio's misplaced quotations from earlier drama (e.g. 'To ride in triumph through *Persepolis*' II. 798) and, again, in the parodying of extravagant language (e.g. Ferentes's imitation of Maurucio in his announcement that the Duke is 'resolu'd to lye forth for the breuiating the prolixity of some superfluous transmigration of the Suns double Cadence to the western Horizon', II. 992–4)—when one has said this, one has defended the subplots as far as Ford's ever can be defended (except in *'Tis Pitty*).

Fourthly, I think it should be pointed out that *Loves Sacrifice* is probably a much better play on the stage. The final scene would gain a certain effect from the unexpectedness of Fernando's appearance; there are throughout, as elsewhere in Ford, some significant silences, which are apt to be missed in reading; and there is much irony, as in *The Broken Heart*, of which an actor could make the most. A good example might be the Duke's words after he has first heard of Fernando's association with Biancha: 'Come mine owne best *Fernando*, my deere friend', Fernando having not the least idea of what the words mean to the Duke, and to the audience. (III. 1806)

Then let it be clearly said that whatever one may think of *Loves Sacrifice* as a whole, there are many memorable scenes and passages, almost enough to 'atone', to use Hartley Coleridge's word, for most faults.

One particularly interesting feature of the characterization of the Duke is the stress Ford puts on his constant awareness of the fact that he married beneath his rank when he married Biancha, an awareness which the dramatist seems to see as the weakness in the Duke's armour. At first he congratulates himself on his courage and liberality of mind in marrying against the wishes of his counsellors; then, when he hears of her faithlessness, he thinks naturally of her origin:

> *Biancha*! why, I tooke her
> From lower then a bondage; hell of hels?
>
> (III. 1791–2)

(Acute psychological observation, rather than Burton, must account for touches like that.)

Naturally, then, this weak link gives Fiormonda an opening when she wishes to taunt the Duke with his disgrace:

*Fior.*  Art thou *Caraffa*? is there in thy veynes
One drop of blood that issued from the loynes
Of *Pauy's* ancient Dukes? or dost thou sit
On great *Lorenzo's* seat, our glorious father,
And canst not blush to be so farre beneath
The spirit of Heroicke ancestors?
Canst thou ingrosse a slauish shame? which men,
Far far below the Region of thy state,
Not more abhorre, then study to reuenge.
Thou an Italian? I could burst with rage,
To thinke I haue a brother so befool'd,
In giuing patience to a harlots lust.

*R.D.*  One, my Lord, that doth so palpably, so apparantly
make her Adulteries a Trophey, whiles the poting-sticke
to her vnsatiate and more then goatish abomination,
jeeres at, and flouts your sleepish, and more then
sleepish security.

*Fior.*  What is she, but the sallow-coloured brat
Of some vnlanded banckrupt? taught to catch
The easie fancies of young prodigall bloods,

In springes of her stewe-instructed Art? Here's your most
Vertous Dutchesse, your rare peece.

R.D.    More base in the infinitenesse of her sensuality,
Then corruption can infect: to clip and inueagle
Your friend too, oh vnsufferable! A friend? how of
All men are you most vnfortunate? to poure out
Your soule into the bosome of such a creature,
As holds it Religion to make your owne trust a key,
To open the passage to your owne wiues wombe,
To be drunke in the priuacies of your bed:
Thinke vpon that, Sir.

Duke    Be gentle in your tortures, ee'ne for pitty;
For pitty's cause I begge it.

Fior.    Be a Prince?
Th'hadst better, Duke, thou hadst bin borne a peasant.
Now boyes will sing thy scandall in the streets,
Tune Ballads to thy infamy, get mony
By making Pageants of thee, and inuent
Some strangely-shap'd *man-beast*, that may for hornes
Resemble thee, and call it *Pawy's* Duke.

Duke    Endlesse immortall plague.

R.D.    There's the mischiefe, Sir:
In the meane time you shall bee sure to haue a
Bastard, (of whom you did not so much as beget a little
toe, a left eare, or halfe the further side of an
vpper lip) inherit both your Throne and Name; this
would kill the soule of very patience it selfe.

Duke    Forbeare.

(IV. 1907-53)

There are few finer scenes in Ford than this. The rhetorical
force of Fiormonda is magnificently balanced by the glibness of
D'avolos to give something of the effect of a musical composition in which the bass mockingly echoes the treble; and to get
the effect not only is all Ford's poetic power necessary but also
the skill in prose that is not so often shown. (Obviously all
D'avolos's speeches here should be printed as prose.) The reduction of the usually voluble and haughty Duke to a state in which
he can only stammer out his humble plea to them to be merciful
adds the final touch of characterization that makes the scene
memorable.

Another whole scene in which the characterization holds
one's attention is that in Act I in which Fernando is first left
alone with Fiormonda. D'avolos has just told him of her pas-

sion, which Fernando certainly does not return; and it is an interesting battle of tactics as he tries to keep her off the subject by talking of her dead husband, while she makes open advances to him.

Finally, there are again and again in the play those 'swift revelations of character in a phrase' which some have denied to Ford but which I should list among his greatest merits. I remember Biancha's brave defiance of the Duke as, sword in hand, he rejects her protestations and demands to know why he has been deceived:

> I tell yee, if you needs would be resolu'd,
> I held *Fernando* much the properer man
> (v. 2432–3);

the Duke's later agony when he learns that the wife he has killed was chaste:

> *Biancha* chaste,
> Had not the furie of some hellish rage
> Blinded all reasons sight, I might haue seene
> Her clearenesse in her confidence to dye
> (v. 2659–62);

in the final scene Fernando's taunting of the Duke:

> Com'st thou, *Caraffa*,
> To practise yet a rape vpon the dead?
> (v. 2768–9)

and the Duke's dying words:

> So; I grow sweetly empty; all the pipes
> Of life vn-vessell life
> (v. 2838–9).

Yet no one, I take it, would deny the faults of the play. Too much of it is merely theatrical, in the worse sense, and written without any great interest; and too much of it is conventional. Fernando's soliloquy on his love for Biancha, in Act II, and his distraction when D'avolos shows him her picture, in the hope that he will give himself away, are not of the same order of dramatic merit as his first interview with Fiormonda; Fiormonda's passionate desire to have Fernando love her is not explained and accords ill with the Fiormonda of Act IV; her final words represent merely the conventional unmotivated repentance; and generally the last act is always on the verge of bathos.

*Loves Sacrifice* is not one of Ford's great plays, and I find it difficult to understand why Havelock Ellis should have included it in his 'Mermaid' Ford instead of *The Ladies Triall*. But it may have been the experimenting in both it and *The Queen* with the reworking of a Shakespearian plot that made possible *'Tis Pitty* and marked the transition from the complex plots of *The Lovers Melancholy* and *The Broken Heart* to the greater dramatic simplicity of the play I believe to be superior to either.

## VII

## 'Tis Pitty Shee's a Whore

IN 'TIS PITTY Ford reaches what is probably his highest point as a dramatist. Others of his plays may be as fine or even finer in single scenes, but here for the first time he seems not to need to rely on previous literature for his ideas of how characters will act in given situations.

Yet it is characteristic of his method of working that this, in a way his most independent and original play, would seem to have begun as a reworking of a Shakespearian tragedy, *Romeo and Juliet*. Shakespeare's lovers were divided and brought to their deaths primarily because of the enmity of their families; their difficulties, one might say, are external (in spite of the occasional suggestions that Shakespeare was working towards his later view of tragedy as the outcome of character). Ford's is the tragedy of two lovers whose union is finally impossible because of an internal impediment: they are brother and sister. One might say that *'Tis Pitty* is a variation on the theme of *Romeo and Juliet* as *Loves Sacrifice* is a variation on the theme of *Othello*; and there are also correspondences of situation, character and phrasing.

For example, in Ford's play as in Shakespeare's there is a Friar who acts as adviser to the lovers (in *'Tis Pitty*, to Giovanni mainly) and at whose cell the marriage of the heroine is to take place. Bonaventura is unlike Friar Laurence in temperament but sometimes uses words that echo other characters in *Romeo and Juliet*: for instance, his advice to Giovanni that there are 'a thousand faces' that 'shine more glorious' than Annabella's (I. 118–19) is Benvolio's advice to Romeo to 'Examine other beauties' (I. i. 234).

Again, the heroine, Annabella, is attended by a nurse, Putana, of the earth, earthy, who has the same turn of mind and even the same jokes as Juliet's nurse. One may compare, from *Romeo and Juliet*, the nurse's account of her husband's witticism to the infant Juliet:

> doest thou fall vpon thy face? thou wilt fall
> backeward when thou hast more wit
>
> (I. iii. 55–6)

with this from *'Tis Pitty*:

> Annabella.   O *Guardian*, what a Paradise of joy
>                    Haue I past ouer!
> Putana.      Nay what a Paradise of ioy haue you past vnder?
>
> (II. 568–70)

Putana also shares with Juliet's nurse a remarkable ability to put expediency above honour when circumstances are inconvenient, and her 'what though hee be your Brother' (II. 572) recalls immediately 'I thinke it best you married with the Countie' (III. v. 219).

Then Annabella's father, the good-natured Florio, is often like Capulet in his more expansive moods and sometimes echoes Capulet's phrasing. Florio's

> I would not for my wealth, my daughters loue
> Should cause the spilling of one drop of blood
>
> (I. 208–9)

recalls Capulet's

> I would not for the wealth of all the towne,
> Here in my house do him disparagement
>
> (I. v. 71–2);

and Florio's interview with Donado, in which he refuses to put pressure on his only daughter to marry Bergetto:

> I will not force my Daughter 'gainst her will.
> You see I haue but two, a Sonne and Her . . .
> And if she like your Nephew, let him haue her
>
> (I. 439–40, 448)

corresponds with Capulet's first discussion of Juliet with Paris.

Finally, the setting and atmosphere of *'Tis Pitty* is that of *Romeo and Juliet*, although of course there is no need to postulate direct indebtedness here. *'Tis Pitty* is set in Parma, Italy, obviously because Italy seemed to Ford a more likely country for his story of passion and intrigue than, say, the equally significant Sparta of *The Broken Heart*. Sensabaugh points out that to Burton Italy was a country which promoted love-melancholy (p. 26); but the dramatic tradition of Shakespeare and Webster would be at least as important to Ford. At any rate, he goes to

some trouble to establish his background; this Italy is a land
where individual action generally anticipates or replaces justice (that is surely the point of the scene in which the Cardinal
protects Grimaldi from the legal consequences of his murder
of Bergetto) and Vasques says to Soranzo, when Soranzo states
his resolve to quench all his wrongs in blood,

> Now you begin to turne Italian.
>
> (v. 2261)

As in *Romeo and Juliet*, the main action of the play is made more
probable by the violence that surrounds it.

   The difference between *'Tis Pitty* and *The Broken Heart* is
perhaps well suggested by a comparison of their opening scenes.
In *The Broken Heart*, Orgilus's conversation with his father has
the function primarily of exposition, but in *'Tis Pitty* Giovanni's
discussion with the Friar not only tells us what has happened
before but also presents us immediately with the principal
dramatic conflict, between Giovanni's incestuous love and the
established order.

> *Giovanni.*  Shall a peeuish sound,
> A customary forme, from man to man,
> Of brother and of sister, be a barre
> Twixt my perpetuall happinesse and mee?
> Say that we had one father, say one wombe,
> (Curse to my ioyes) gaue both vs life, and birth;
> Are wee not therefore each to other bound
> So much the more by Nature; by the links
> Of blood, of reason; Nay if you will hau't,
> Euen of Religion, to be euer one,
> One soule, one flesh, one loue, one heart, one *All*?
>
> (I. 82–92)

(Gifford duly said, in a note on Act I, scene ii, that the problem
was set forth *too* abruptly, considering the 'revolting nature' of
the plot!) What the dramatist has achieved for the first time is
a beginning that is both striking and relevant.

   Ford presents Giovanni as one who, when he wishes to pursue
a certain course of action, is prepared to find reasons for pursuing it; and he expects the Friar to give him a reason for not
pursuing it. The Friar's only relevant reply is that religion is
above reason—an answer which will never satisfy the ration-
alist. On a man like Giovanni, the Friar's attitude of holding up

his hands in horror and distress will have no lasting effect, and
the well-meant advice that the sinner must pray is bound to
fail. Giovanni characteristically reports to Annabella later that
the Church 'tells mee I may loue you'; the Friar's failure to
prove a case against him is to Giovanni equivalent to condona-
tion. It is not, as some would imply, that the dramatist believes
Giovanni to be right, but that the Friar cannot set him right.
This, then, is the beginning of the tragedy of Giovanni: that the
one he turns to for advice is in the circumstances inadequate,
the moral order has an unworthy representative, and the poten-
tial sinner proceeds with his sin.

Miss Sargeaunt seems to miss the full significance of this when
she writes: 'If we knew more of Ford we might know more of
the Friar, but as it is he must remain, like his creator, something
of an enigma' (p. 126). Friars do not always give good advice,
or become enigmas if they do not give it. Ford's Friar is a weak
person, and it is therefore quite in character for him to decide
later, when things go wrong, to leave the city, to 'shun this
comming blowe' (v. 2219). The only puzzle here has surely been
created in the minds of the critics.

It might be suggested also that the character of the Friar is
the answer to Sensabaugh's difficulty, that Giovanni 'seems,
peculiarly, to have contracted both religious melancholy and
heroical love' (p. 68). Giovanni's religious dissatisfaction is
surely simply a result of his love; it does not occur to him to
question religion until religion runs counter to his passion and
cannot convince him that that passion is wrong.

Giovanni's sister, Annabella, is not so intellectual in her
approach to a problem. The scene in which she is introduced,
in company with her nurse, has the function of pointing this
contrast with Giovanni; and one notices how brief are
Annabella's comments. She does not run as easily as Giovanni
to rhetoric and it is Putana (again like Juliet's nurse) who does
most of the talking. This scene also has the important function
of comparing Giovanni, to his advantage, with Annabella's
other suitors. (The discussion of suitors by heroine and com-
panion reminds one of Julia and Lucetta in *The Two Gentlemen
of Verona* I. ii. and of Portia and Nerissa in *The Merchant of Venice*
I. ii., and it will be seen that the discussion has the same place in

the play in all three cases—immediately after the opening scene
which introduces the love problem of the hero.) The suitors of
Annabella play quite an important part in 'Tis Pitty, and the
story accordingly suffered when Maeterlinck, in his adaptation
of it as Annabella, omitted the subplot of Hippolita. Its function
is to emphasize that even the best of the suitors, Soranzo, is a
philanderer and in many ways unprincipled; and so Ford does
not ask the audience to make its choice between Giovanni and
a blameless eligible candidate for Annabella's hand in marriage.
He does not take up the general moral issue, but adopts the
justifiable course of keeping one's dramatic sympathies with
Giovanni rather than his rivals Grimaldi, Bergetto and Soranzo.

But before the 'subplots' develop, the lovers are brought
together. Giovanni, turning over the problem in his mind, works
himself up to a state of emotional indecision and turmoil—
presented more convincingly than Orgilus's, because it is presented as abnormal and is sooner dropped. Annabella at first
thinks him 'franticke'; but in swift interchange of dialogue the
true nature of Giovanni's passion is revealed to her. It is
interesting to notice again how little Annabella is given to say,
and how it is by avoiding speech rather than by expanding it
that the dramatist suggests the strength of her emotion, her
reticence and the completeness of her surrender when it comes:

> Gio. O *Annabella* I am quite vndone,
> The loue of thee (my sister) and the view
> Of thy immortall beauty hath vntun'd
> All harmony both of my rest and life,
> Why d'ee not strike?
> Anna. Forbid it my iust feares,
> If this be true, 'twere fitter I were dead.
> Gio. True *Annabella*; 'tis no time to iest,
> I haue too long supprest the hidden flames
> That almost haue consum'd me; I haue spent
> Many a silent night in sighes and groanes,
> Ran ouer all my thoughts, despis'd my Fate,
> Reason'd against the reasons of my loue,
> Done all that smooth'd-cheeke Vertue could aduise,
> But found all bootelesse; 'tis my destiny,
> That you must eyther loue, or I must dye.
> Anna. Comes this in sadnesse from you?
> Gio. Let some mischiefe
> Befall me soone, if I dissemble ought.

*Anna.* You are my brother *Giouanni.*

*Gio.* You,
  My Sister *Annabella*; I know this:
  And could afford you instance why to loue
  So much the more for this; to which intent
  Wise Nature first in your Creation ment
  To make you mine: else't had beene sinne and foule,
  To share one beauty to a double soule.
  Neerenesse in birth or blood, doth but perswade
  A neerer neerenesse in affection.
  I haue askt Counsell of the holy Church,
  Who tells mee I may loue you, and 'tis iust,
  That since I may, I should; and will, yes will:
  Must I now liue, or dye?

*Anna.* Liue, thou hast wonne
  The field, and neuer fought; what thou hast vrg'd,
  My captiue heart had long agoe resolu'd.
  I blush to tell thee, (but I'le tell thee now)
  For euery sigh that thou hast spent for me,
  I haue sigh'd ten; for euery teare shed twenty:
  And not so much for that I lou'd, as that
  I durst not say I lou'd; nor scarcely thinke it.

(I. 374–414)

At the beginning of Act II, then, Giovanni is seen in the role
of the successful lover, elated, teasing Annabella and finding a
ready response from her; he is even prepared to raise for a
moment, half seriously, the question of her marriage to another.

*Gio.* But I shall lose you *Sweet-heart.*
*Anna.* But you shall not.
*Gio.*     You must be married Mistres.
*Anna.* Yes, to whom?
*Gio.*    Some one must haue you.
*Anna.* You must.
*Gio.*    Nay some other.
*Anna.* Now prithee do not speake so, without iesting
  You'le make me weepe in earnest.
*Gio.* What you will not.
  But tell me sweete, can'st thou be dar'd to sweare
  That thou wilt liue to mee, and to no other?
*Anna.* By both our loues I dare.

(II. 546–55)

It is quite different when the subject is raised by somebody
else. Giovanni tells the horrified Friar of his winning of
Annabella and brushes away objections:

> Your age o're rules you, had you youth like mine,
> You'd make her loue your heauen, and her diuine.
>
> (II. 940–1)

The Friar suggests that Annabella should marry, and it is Giovanni's turn to be shocked:

> Marriage? why that's to dambe her; that's to proue
> Her greedy of variety of lust
>
> (II. 946–7)

—surely two of the most memorable lines in English drama.

Then the action accelerates. Annabella has to give an answer to Soranzo's proposal of marriage. She is firm in her rejection of him, but (like Juliet) is not above the deliberately ambiguous

> If I hereafter finde that I must marry,
> It shall be you or none.
>
> (III. 1228–9)

But those lines are to have ironically a further, a third, meaning that is not in Annabella's mind when she speaks them. She is soon discovered to be with child; and the Friar, after torturing her, characteristically, with pictures of the Hell that awaits sinners, can only suggest that she marry Soranzo. Annabella, distraught, agrees.

The scene of the marriage feast and of the poisoning of Soranzo's former mistress, Hippolita, serves to remind the audience that Soranzo is far from blameless. Otherwise his position— he knows nothing of the pregnancy and of the real feeling of the woman he is marrying—might swing sympathy entirely away from Annabella and Giovanni. But as it is, the conflict is between two wrongs; and the balance is beautifully held in the scene in which Soranzo learns of Annabella's pregnancy. He acts cruelly, but credibly; Annabella's devotion to Giovanni (whose name is not betrayed) makes her anger him even more; and the scene is saved from melodrama not only by its probability but also by the touches of real pathos which are introduced. That Ford is not without sympathy even for Soranzo is suggested well enough, for example, by Annabella's admission to him:

> I must confesse, I know you lou'd mee well.
>
> (IV. 1906)

Putana is worked upon by Soranzo's servant, Vasques, to

reveal the name of Annabella's lover (it will be seen that the
minor characters in this play all have their functions in the
main plot) and Soranzo plans to take his revenge at a banquet
he will give to celebrate his birthday. Annabella manages to
warn Giovanni, through the Friar; and the play reaches its
climax in the final meeting of the lovers, at the beginning of the
fifth act.

Giovanni, always prone to hastiness in action as to rhetoric in
speech, is in a dangerous mood; Annabella, not having so simple
an outlet for her emotions, is quieter. The contrast between the
two is poignant here as Giovanni proceeds relentlessly on his
determined path:

*Gio.*  What chang'd so soone? hath your new sprightly Lord
Found out a tricke in night-games more then wee
Could know in our simplicity? ha! is't so?
Or does the fitt come on you, to proue treacherous
To your past vowes and oathes?

*Anna.*  Why should you jeast
At my Calamity, without all sence
Of the approaching dangers you are in?

*Gio.*  What danger's halfe so great as thy reuolt?
Thou art a faithlesse sister, else thou know'st,
Malice, or any treachery beside
Would stoope to my bent-browes; why I hold Fate
Clasp't in my fist, and could Command the Course
Of times eternall motion; hadst thou beene
One thought more steddy then an ebbing Sea.
And what? you'le now be honest, that's resolu'd?

*Anna.*  Brother, deare brother, know what I haue beene,
And know that now there's but a dying time
Twixt vs and our Confusion: let's not waste
These precious houres in vayne and vselesse speech.
Alas, these gay attyres were not put on
But to some end; this suddaine solemne Feast
Was not ordayn'd to riott in expence;
I that haue now beene chambred here alone,
Bard of my Guardian, or of any else,
Am not for nothing at an instant free'd
To fresh accesse; be not deceiu'd *My Brother*,
This Banquet is an harbinger of Death
To you and mee, resolue your selfe it is,
And be prepar'd to welcome it.

(v. 2300–29)

Gradually Giovanni comes to the point, Annabella at first

feeling that he should be *doing* more (it is the Romeo-Juliet contrast, incidentally); but as she sees that he means to kill her, it is noticeable again that she is given less and less to say. It is merely:

> Then I see your drift,
> Yee blessed Angels, guard mee
>
> (v. 2377-8);

then, in answer to his 'forgiue mee',

> With my heart
>
> (2391);

next, when she sees the dagger

> What meanes this?
>
> (2399);

followed by one exclamation of distress after the stroke:

> Oh brother by your hand?
>
> (2403)

and the dying words:

> Forgiue him Heauen——and me my sinnes, farwell.
> Brother vnkind, vnkind——mercy great Heauen——oh——oh
>
> (2409-10)

Giovanni in comparison is hysterical, almost but not quite anti-pathetic. He kills her to save her further torture.

I used to think that in the following scene, when Giovanni comes to the banquet with Annabella's bleeding heart upon his dagger, stabs Soranzo and is himself murdered, Ford was simply descending to melodrama, accepting the bad dramatic traditions of the appropriate ending for a tragedy of blood.[1] But now I am not so sure. Ford had the authority of Burton, if he needed it, for believing that men acted thus under the influence of heroical love. But did he need that authority? It is a common-place of psychology that the thinker, forced to play the part of the man of action, often acts rashly, even overacts his part; and I believe that Ford is here presenting Govanni's actions as those natural to a man of his temperament faced with a situation that seems to him to demand that something be done. And this, incidentally, would complete the correspondence with *Romeo and Juliet*, where Romeo is by nature the thinker, even the

---

[1] I had noted, for example, that Gismunda was presented with a cup of gold, with her lover's 'bloody heart reeking hot in it' in the old Inner Temple play of *Tancred and Gismunda*.

dreamer, but, forced to action, is far more dangerous than all
the Tybalts and Mercutios; his creed becomes

> Away to heauen, respectiue Lenitie,
> And fire and Fury, be my conduct now.
>
> (III. i. 128-9)

and to Romeo in this mood Paris seems a mere ineffective youth,
to be dissuaded from danger but to be removed without scruple
if he will not take the hint.

What this means, then, is that Ford is faced with the problem
of showing on the stage a character who in real life would act
melodramatically. He had to give a realistic presentation of
melodramatic action; it has seemed to many a melodramatic
presentation of reality. The difference, in drama, is very slight;
and Eugene O'Neill, faced with the same problem in *Anna
Christie*, confessed that he could not solve it.

In any case, Giovanni is not a completely unsympathetic
figure at the end. If now he holds Fate clasped in his fist, he
knows that it is only because he has made his own death
inevitable; he faces it, without illusion, and to the Cardinal's

> Thinke on thy life and end, and call for mercy

replies with

> *Mercy?* why I haue found it in this *Iustice.*
>
> (v. 2540-1)

The last word on his lips is the name of Annabella.

It is, then, surely a mark of Ford's dramatic skill and not of
his moral aberration that we should wish so heartily to agree
with the final couplet of the play, spoken, be it noted, by the
Cardinal:

> *Of one* so young, so rich in Natures store,
> Who could not say, '*Tis pitty shee's a Whore?*

It is both irrelevant and misleading for *The Cambridge History
of English Literature*[2] to brand this 'an assault at once so insidious
and so daring upon the foundations of accepted morality'. Yet
that confusion runs through most of the criticism of the play,
from Vernon Lee's discussion of 'this miserable, morbid, com-
passionated Giovanni'[3] to Sherman's elaborate attempt to
deduce from it that Ford was an ardent believer in free love:

---

[2]Vol. vi. ch. 8 (by W. A. Neilson).     [3]*Euphorion* (London, 1884) i, 102.

The tragic quality of the situation in Forde's eyes, is not at all the fearful moral aberration of this brother and sister. The tragic quality to him is the malign accident that these two enamoured souls should have taken lodging in the bodies of brother and sister. Their loves are pure; their souls unstained ... It is the impure, material universe at cross purposes with the heart, that causes their tragedy. It is impossible not to feel beneath the words of Giovanni the sentiments of Forde. He draws this hero and heroine as if he loved them. He gives them all the fine situations, the poetical imagination, the steadfastness, the noble sentiments, the starry aspirations. He strives as much as he can to put them in the right and the world in the wrong. He crowns their adulterous and incestuous love with roses, and attempts to irradiate their crime with celestial light.[4]

What Ford crowns the love of Annabella and Giovanni with, one must protest, is not roses but death. And there is no reason why he should not grant them poetical imaginations, steadfastness and so on. Othello has all those qualities too, but nobody argues from this that Shakespeare approved of wife-murder. Ford is perfectly entitled to present incestuous love as the tragic flaw in otherwise admirable characters.

Yet Sensabaugh echoes Sherman's sentiment in his analysis of Ford's plays:

The whole meaning of Ford's plays, in fact, rests on the supremacy of love over all, on the belief that beauty and love should command more respect than convention and law; he could not brook custom that might judge against beauty, or conceive any crisis of unsatisfied passion, adultery, or incest where love should not conquer. (p. 65)

But neither Sherman nor Sensabaugh, I believe, can produce evidence from the plays (how can one ever produce such evidence from any *play*?) that Ford believed love ought to conquer. What Ford has done is to present an example where love in fact did not conquer; as Sensabaugh elsewhere (p. 175) admits, he presents in his tragedies 'unresolvable dilemmas'. And it seems to me the height of perversity to mention *Christes Bloodie Sweat* and *A Line of Life* as showing 'a knowledge of Christian and of classical thought' without adding, which is true, that they proclaim an approval of it, and yet to infer from the plays the very opposite.

Not, of course, that the inference is right. To be sure, *Giovanni* says of Annabella:

[4]Bang, *Materialien*, xxiii. p. xii.

> if euer after times should heare
> Of our fast-knit affections, though perhaps
> The Lawes of *Conscience* and of *Ciuill vse*
> May iustly blame vs, yet when they but know
> Our loues, *That loue* will wipe away that rigour,
> Which would in other *Incests* bee abhorr'd.
>
> (v. 2380–5)

Miss Sargeaunt comments that this may be only a revival of the old Romantic idea that great love is its own justification. What Giovanni says, of course, is not that love is a justification but that it is an alleviation, an alleviation of a sin which can justly be condemned. And Giovanni (or Ford, if you like) may even have had in mind 'Her sins which are many are forgiven—for she loved much'. (Professor F. P. Wilson has well pointed out in *Elizabethan and Jacobean* that there was generally something soundly Christian in Elizabethan and Jacobean 'atheism'.) Giovanni may struggle against the inevitable with his:

> O that it were not in Religion sinne,
> To make our loue a God, and worship it
>
> (i. 300–1)

—but the premise from which he starts is that it is a sin.

It is most regrettable that the merits of this, of all Ford's plays, should have been obscured for so many by misleading commentary, for it is, I believe, one of the finest tragedies out-side Shakespeare. It has, to be sure, its touches of melodrama and just once or twice there is a trace of the old casualness of plot, as in Richardetto's calm suggestion that his niece should become a nun, now that he has no further plans for her, and her equally calm acceptance of the proposal. But nobody has ever doubted the strength of the play; I have argued for its complete validity of characterization; and various attempts to do without the subplots have only proved how fine is the construction. It is a measure of the difference between *'Tis Pitty* and most of Ford's other plays that, whatever may be said against the subplots of those others, in this one there is greatness. The foolish Bergetto, making the most of such poor logic as he has and completely unaware of his limitations ('Dost take me for a child Poggio?'), becomes a pathetic and almost tragic figure, and his death is not the least of the many great scenes in the play.

It is difficult to see, in view of Ford's development so far, in what ways he could have progressed beyond *'Tis Pitty*. Perhaps because he felt this difficulty himself, he seems to have turned aside to a different kind of drama again; from this, his *Tragicall Historie of Romeo and Juliet*, he turned to historical tragedy, and in *Perkin Warbeck* found still more countries to conquer. But the conquest this time was not complete.

# VIII

## The Chronicle Historie of Perkin Warbeck

PERKIN WARBECK, entered on the Stationers' Register and published in 1634, was never, I believe, thought to be Ford's best play until Mr T. S. Eliot argued that it 'is unquestionably Ford's greatest achievement', if only because 'here for once there is no lapse of taste or judgment'.[1] Mr Eliot's views must always be carefully considered and can rarely be rejected; but it does seem that there is a certain seeking for novelty in his revaluations of Elizabethan playwrights (as in his equally surprising claim that *Sophonisba* shows Marston at his best) and I do question whether here he is arguing along the right lines. I am not the first to suggest that he has underrated *'Tis Pitty* (Clifford Bax[2] and Miss Sargeaunt are only two who have opposed him on that question); and in suggesting that he has therefore overrated *Perkin Warbeck*, I merely return to what has been the common view of the play.

Havelock Ellis was surely nearer the truth when he said of Ford's only history:

> In *Perkin Warbeck* he laid aside his characteristic defects, and also his characteristic merits, to achieve a distinct dramatic success. It is the least interesting of his plays for those who care for the peculiar qualities which mark Ford's genius, but it ranks among our best historical dramas. Ford's interest in psychological problems may be detected in his impartial, even sympathetic, treatment of Warbeck; but for the most part this play is an exception to every generalisation that may be arrived at concerning his work.[3]

In his suggestion that it is 'the least interesting of Ford's plays . . .' Ellis no doubt went too far; Professor Ellis-Fermor seems to put the case better when she says simply: 'Like *Edward II* in the series of Marlowe's plays, it is likely to please best those who least appreciate the author's individual flavour' (p.233).

[1] *Elizabethan Essays*, p. 146.
[2] *T.L.S.*, 12 May 1932, p. 351.
[3] *John Ford*, pp. xii–xiii.

One would have said without reading the play that history would be likely to cramp Ford's genius. Why then did he write a chronicle?

The fullest attempt to answer this question has been perhaps Dr Struble's. In her *Critical Edition of Ford's 'Perkin Warbeck'*[4] she argues that he had a special interest in the subject from the point of view of political theory and so set out to contrast the Tudor theory of sovereignty with the Stuart belief in divine right and infallibility. She is able to quote incidental comments from the play—single lines and short passages—which may seem to support her contention; but that any playgoer ever came away from *Perkin Warbeck* feeling that he had learnt something of political theory, I find it impossible to believe. Dr Struble also thinks that *Perkin Warbeck* was 'obviously designed to fill the gap between *Richard III* and *Henry VIII*' (p .16). But this too is far from obvious to me. There is no evidence for it either in the text or elsewhere; the play is not, after all, called *Henry VII* and is not a record of the King's reign; and so far from filling a gap between Shakespeare's histories, it would falsify the plan of the *Henry VI* trilogy, later filled in by the *Richard II*, *Henry IV* and *Henry V* group, by showing that in fact Richmond's accession did not end the contention between York and Lancaster (as the lengthy exposition in Act I makes clear).

Why then did Ford write it? There is probably no one explanation. I do think it likely that Ford, as a student of history and literary history and an admirer of Shakespeare, had a certain interest in trying to continue the great tradition of chronicle plays established by Greene, Peele, Marlowe and Shakespeare; but I believe that his main interest in the play could have been as a problem of technique. Mr Charles Morgan has recently adapted Wordsworth's famous statement about the sonnet and has told us that to him, as novelist,

> In sundry moods, 'twas pastime to be bound
> Within the stage's scanty plot of ground.[5]

An experienced dramatist (and *Perkin Warbeck* comes after the main group of Ford's plays) might similarly wish to meet the challenge offered by the restriction of historical drama. In both

[4]pp. 30–37.
[5]*The Flashing Stream* (London, 1938) p. xxi.

these senses, then, *Perkin Warbeck* may have been to Ford a labour of love.

He seems to me to say as much in the Prologue, one of his best:

> Studyes haue, of this Nature, been of late
> So out of fashion, so vnfollow'd; that
> It is become more Iustice, to reviue
> The antick follyes of the Times, then striue
> To countenance wise Industrie: no want
> Of Art, doth render witt, or lame, or scant,
> Or slothfull, in the purchase of fresh bayes;
> But want of Truth in Them, who giue the prayse
> To their selfe-loue, presuming to out-doe
> The *Writer*, or (for need) the *Actor's* too.
> But such THIS AVTHOVR'S silence best befitt's,
> Who bidd's Them, be in loue, with their owne witt's:
> From *Him*, to cleerer Iudgement's, wee can say,
> Hee shew's a Historie, couch't in a Play:
> A Historie of noble mention, knowne,
> Famous, and true: most noble, 'cause our owne:
> Not forg'd from *Italie*, from *Fraunce*, from *Spaine*,
> But Chronicled at *Home*; as rich in strayne
> Of braue Attempts, as ever, fertile Rage
> In Action, could beget to grace the Stage.
> Wee cannot limitt *Scenes*, for the whole Land
> It selfe, appeard too narrow to with-stand
> *Competitors for Kingdomes*: nor is heere
> Vnnecessary mirth forc't, to indeere
> A multitude; on *these two*, rest's the Fate
> Of worthy expectation; TRVTH and STATE.

'Truth and State', then, were his aim. Gifford (p. 128) early noted the dignity of the play, which is quite free from Elizabethan rant (there may be guns, in Meleander's phrase, but there is no pompous whining); and Brereton and Pickburn, in their edition, speak of it as 'statuesque'.[6] The play has something of the tone of *The Lovers Melancholy* and is quite free, as the Prologue says, from *unnecessary* mirth. There are comic characters, namely Perkin's attendants, but they are drawn quietly and are kept in the background. (One does not forget that 'wise formalitie' John a Water, Mayor of Cork, whose speech is so circumspect and circumlocutious that he does not make a single positive statement in the course of the play.)

[6] *Ford's 'Perkin Warbeck'* (Sydney, 1896) p. xiii.

Ford achieved his 'State'. But what of the 'Truth'? It has
been found that he was very careful and collated Bacon's
*History of King Henry the Seventh* (1622) and Gainsford's *True and
Wonderful Historie of Perkin Warbeck* (1618) and possibly Hall and
Holinshed. (Gainsford really covers Hall and Holinshed; the
earlier writers, like Brereton, who thought Ford relied on them
did not know of his debt to Gainsford, which was first analysed
by Dr Struble.[7]) These authorities Ford often followed closely,
even to the point of versifying their prose, somewhat in
Shakespeare's manner. But he also, like Shakespeare, altered
history for dramatic purposes. He re-arranged and compressed
(for example, two Scottish attacks on the North of England are
made into one); Daliell, although mentioned in a source, is a
fictitious character; and Katherine, who in fact married again
three times, is made to swear to Warbeck in the play that she
will 'dye a faithfull widdow to thy bed' (v. 2708) and the
audience is told nothing to the contrary. Moreover, Perkin
Warbeck did in fact confess that he was an impostor.

Why did Ford not let him do so? The answer of Miss
Cochnower is: 'Possibly . . . he let this typical treatment run on
until it occurred to him that it would be easier, and rather smart,
to remain silent concerning his own opinion.'[8] No doubt all
criticism involves the risk of reducing the subject of the criticism to the critic's own level; but one cannot help feeling that
Miss Cochnower might have been rather less anxious to brand
a great dramatist as merely 'smart' and to find in a legitimate
dramatic device 'something of cheap naughtiness'.

Quite clearly Ford is interested in Perkin Warbeck's mind.
He gives the key to his interpretation of him when Pretender
and King first meet; Dawbney and the other bystanders wonder
that the King lets Perkin talk so much, but Henry is happy to
let him run on:

> O let him range:
> The player's on the stage still, 'tis his part;
> A' does but act.
>
> (v. 2438–40)

To Warbeck himself Henry speaks in the same way:

[7] *Anglia*, xlix (1926), 80–91.
[8] 'John Ford' in Shafer ed. *Seventeenth Century Studies* (Princeton 1933) i. 226.

> thus, *your Aunt of Burgundie,*
> Your *Dutchesse Aunt* enform'd her Nephew; so
> The lesson prompted, and well conn'd, was moulded
> Into familiar Dialogue, oft rehearsed,
> Till learnt by heart, 'tis now, receiv'd for truth.
> (v. 2446–50)

A little later, he sums it up:

> The custome sure of being stil'd *a King,*
> Hath fastend in his thought that HE IS SVCH.
> (v. 2504–5)

Warbeck, then, is no Hamlet. He is not the kind of man who reasons things out, and he is capable of all forms of self-deception. It is less surprising, therefore, that Ford gives him not one soliloquy. As a matter of fact, Ford uses soliloquy very rarely indeed, particularly for a psychological dramatist. He prefers to bring out character by more truly dramatic methods, prefers the half-muttered comment to the full self-exposition. With a man like Warbeck, soliloquy might have had little value anyway, because he would not be clear to himself. And if he had been certain of the reasons for his imposture, in soliloquy he would have given himself away. Now Ford does not give the *facts* about Warbeck until the very end of the play, when Lambert Simnell tells him and the audience that his pedigree has been 'publisht':

> you are knowne
> For *Osbecks* sonne of *Turney,* a loose runnagate,
> A Landloper: your Father was a *Iewe,*
> Turn'd Christian meerely to repayre his miseries.
> (v. 2575–8)

Until this point of the action, there is always the theoretic possibility that Warbeck has a genuine claim to the throne; and so by not making it certain that Warbeck is an impostor, Ford preserves such conflict as the play has, as a real conflict: one claimant to the throne opposes another.

What this means, however, is that the dramatist has deliberately restricted himself in the drawing of Warbeck, so far as his claims to the throne are concerned. He does not wish to make it certain that Warbeck will fail (although, of course, with a chronicle play, the dramatist is often handicapped by the audience's preknowledge of the outcome). On the other hand, Ford does wish to make it highly improbable that Warbeck could have just claims. The audience's sympathy must not be too much with him. Ford's answer to the problem—and it is a splendid one—is to portray Warbeck indirectly, to make him appear in the wrong by making Henry so obviously in the right and by showing the class of man to whom the Pretender's cause appeals.

Accordingly, Ford is careful to present Henry all the time as the ideal monarch. He is always dignified, impressive; he keeps the reins in his own hands and his nobles can tell him little that he does not already know; he is merciful wherever possible but not sentimentally slow in action, although astute enough not to appear before Stanley when that former friend is being led to execution. And this monarch refuses even to take Perkin Warbeck seriously:

> phew, hee's but a running weede,
> At pleasure to be pluck'd vp by the rootes.
> (I. 300–1)

Nobody both disinterested and intelligent ever believes Warbeck's claims. James of Scotland is pleased to have a weapon against England but is quick to change sides when England's offers are more profitable; and Stanley's treachery may be only an insurance policy. The real followers of Warbeck are the 'abject scumme of mankinde', as Frion calls them (II. 1160). In Clifford's words

> never had *Counterfeit*
> Such a confused rabble of lost Banquerouts
> For Counsellors.
> (I. 570–2)

Heron, Sketon, John a Water and Astly, a splendidly drawn quartet of 'Muddie-braynd peasants' (II. 1161) thus certainly justify their existence in the play, which therefore shares with *'Tis Pitty* the distinction of having a subplot which no reader of Ford would willingly do without.

Warbeck, then, receives none of our political sympathy. But personally he is attractive, and this discrepancy—ambivalence one might almost call it—gives the play its main character interest. (Internal conflict is not, however, the subject of *Perkin Warbeck*. The only dramatic conflict, one must repeat, is external, between Warbeck and King Henry. And since they do not meet until late in the play, there is an over-extensive use of alternating scenes in the early acts. We pass too often from England to Scotland and back again.)

When we first meet Warbeck (it is not until Act II) we see in his speech the true grace and eloquence of the man. James comments:

> Hee must bee more then subject, who can vtter
> The language of a King, and such is thine.
>
> (II. 772–3)

Crawford, too, is impressed in spite of himself and tells Daliell so:

> Tis more then strange, my reason cannot answere
> Such argument of fine Imposture, couch
> In witch-craft of perswasion, that it fashions
> Impossibilities, as if appearance
> Could cozen *truth it selfe*; this Duk-ling Mushrome
> Hath doubtlesse charm'd the King.
>
> (II. 971–6)

And once Katherine has heard him speak, she is already won:

> Beshrew mee, but his words haue touchd mee home,
> As if his cause concerned mee; I should pittie him
> If a' should proue another then hee seemes.
>
> (II. 788–90)

Thereafter, the question whether he is an impostor or not could almost be said to be irrelevant to her.

It is these qualities—Warbeck's romantic charm, so brilliantly conveyed by the dramatist in his speeches, and Katherine's constancy to him—which make them for the rest of the play, in Katherine's own phrase,

> spectacles to time, and pittie.
>
> (V. 2279)

She never leaves him, even when, having exhausted the King's patience by his second attempt to escape, he is put in the stocks.

> *Oxford.*   Remember (Ladie) who you are; come from
>             That impudent Imposter!
> *Katherine.*        You abuse vs:
>             For when the holy *Church-man* joynd our hands,
>             Our Vowes were reall then; the Ceremonie
>             Was not in apparition, but in act.
>
> (V. 2666–70)

Similarly, Warbeck retains his charm and a certain plausibility until the end. Lambert Simnell's attempts to point out to him the follies of imposture are hopeless, and he dies triumphant:

> Death? pish, 'tis but a sound; a name of ayre;
> A minutes storme; or not so much; to tumble
> From bed to bed, be massacred aliue
> By some *Physitians*, for a moneth, or two,
> In hope of freedome from a Feavers torments,
> Might stagger manhood; here, the paine is past
> Ere sensibly 'tis felt. Be men of spirit!
> Spurne coward passion! so illustrious mention,
> Shall blaze *our names*, and stile vs KINGS O'RE DEATH
>                                      (v. 2761–9)

But the revelation of people like Katherine and Warbeck (in his private capacity) cannot be the main aim of a chronicle and that is one reason for the constant inability of dramatists to turn history into great drama. Shakespeare himself could sometimes only compromise. He made *Henry V* a glorious pageant rather than a great play and gave *Henry IV* added character interest largely through the strictly unhistorical Falstaff. Ford adopted neither of these solutions; and I am not convinced that Miss Sargeaunt has found the right explanation for his refusal to write a chronicle pageant of England's greatness:

Ford is not really concerned at all with the fortune of England, with its traditions, its politics, and its countryside; of these he treats solely because of their effects on the somewhat fantastic character, as he has conceived it, that chance has called on to play a leading part for a short while in the historical scene. (p. 69)

Is it not rather that Ford sees that civil wars are to be regretted not because they hurt abstractions but because they bring death and misery to people who are equally part of England? That would explain why there is no real villain in the play, unless it be Warbeck's secretary, Frion. Instead, there are only, so far as the main characters are concerned, people who are misguided. To show their tragedy may be in a way a better, a truer account of England's history than the picture of England's fortunes that Miss Sargeaunt thinks Ford could not or would not give. *Perkin Warbeck* in its own way is just as patriotic as *Henry V*.

But is all this enough to make a great play? If it is not, it is precisely because human miseries tend to become subordinate

even in *Perkin Warbeck* to wider issues. Ford can show brilliantly
the personal grief of Henry when he learns that his most trusted
counsellor Stanley, 'the *all* of *all* I am' (I. 624), is a traitor.
Equally he can draw a most attractive picture of the gruff
honest Huntley and his relations with Daliell, the man who
should have been his son-in-law. The character of Huntley, too,
is Ford's own invention; and the conversation in Act I between
him and Daliell is Ford's best version yet of the suitor speaking
to the father, or brother, of the woman he loves. As pathetic
as any situation in *The Broken Heart* is Huntley's apology to
Daliell after James has persuaded the willing Katherine to
marry Warbeck, and his grief as much as Calantha's illustrates
that it is the silent griefs that cut the heart strings, as he laments

> I doted
> On every hayre that grew to trim her head
> (III. 1336–7)

but is at least as much concerned at 'the rape done on mine
honor' (III. 1353) by her marriage to Warbeck. There is more
tragedy in Huntley's words than James thinks when to James's
request for prayer for the success of the Scottish army in battle
he replies:

> Prayers are the weapons,
> Which men, so neere their graues as I, doe vse.
> I've little else to doe.
> (III. 1438–40)

But the griefs of subjects, one must repeat, though caused by
history and though the real interest of history to a man like
Ford, must take second place in a true 'Chronicle Historie'. And
what that means is that Ford himself is pushed into the background.

It is difficult, then, to accept Mr Eliot's revaluation of *Perkin
Warbeck*, even granting the play's comparative freedom from
lapses in taste; it is equally difficult to agree with Miss C. V.
Wedgwood[9] that 'it is the best constructed and the most ably
sustained play that he ever wrote'. The constructional merits of
*Perkin Warbeck* are not as great as those of *'Tis Pitty*, although
the historical framework may make them seem so. For what
*Perkin Warbeck* lacks, to quote *The Cambridge History of English*

[9]'John Ford' in *Penguin New Writing* No. 38, p. 99.

*Literature,* is a certain intensity, though 'on the whole it is unmistakably a workmanlike performance'.[10] There are dull passages in it, even if it also contains some of his finest poetry; and Ford cannot give all his attention to the states of mind the portrayal of which is his real strength.

[10]Vol. vi, ch. 8.

## IX

## *The Fancies Chast and Noble* and *The Ladies Triall*

FORD'S last two plays, although not histories, both illustrate as does *Perkin Warbeck* the difficulty he found in constructing a play which should give him ample opportunity for exposition of character and have a plot which would hold interest to the the end. In one of them, *The Fancies*, he sacrificed character to surprise of plot; and the result is a play which has been condemned, not only by those who find it 'coarse and prurient'[1] but also by others, as 'by far Ford's worst'.[2] In the other, *The Ladies Triall*, he essayed the alternative, sacrificing plot to exposition of character—and found himself going beyond the limits of what drama could conveniently express.

*The Fancies* was not published until 1638 but must have been written by the end of 1636, for in that year the Queen's Men left the Phoenix where, according to the title-page, they acted this play.[3] I should be surprised to learn that it was not popular, for in spite of the Prologue it seems more than any other of Ford's plays to have been written down to popular taste.

The Prologue is in the usual vein:

> *The Fancies!* that's our Play; in it is showne
> Nothing, but what our *Author* knowes his *owne*
> Without a *learned theft*; no servant here
> To some *faire Mistris*, borrowes for his eare,
> His locke, his belt, his sword, the fancied grace
> Of any pretty ribon; nor in place
> Of charitable friendship, is brought in
> A thriving *Gamester*, that doth chance to win
> A lusty summe, while the good hand doth ply him,
> And *Fancies*, this, or that, to him sits by him.
> His free invention runnes but in conceit
> Of meere imaginations: there's the hight
> Of what *he* writes, which if traduc'd by some,
> 'Tis well (he sayes) he's farre enough from home.

---

[1]Schelling and Black, *Typical Elizabethan Plays*, p. 900.
[2]Sargeaunt, p. 76; cf. T. S. Eliot who comments on its 'prurient flirting with impropriety' and finds it 'the worst play which Ford himself ever wrote' (*Elizabethan Essays*, p. 140).
[3]Bentley, i. 238–9.

> For *you*, for *him*, for *us*, then this remaines;
> Fancie, your even opinions, for our paines.

The first of the claims here advanced, that the play is the
dramatist's original work, may be granted, but not, I think, the
other two: that it is not conventional and that the dramatist is
above caring what the audience thinks. For although the play
was no doubt something of an experiment in the way of plot—
I should call it a tragi-comedy did I not feel that the classifica-
tion of Ford's plays according to the usual modes is completely
misleading—it was an experiment along lines that were known
to please, and there is much in it that is conventional in the
worst Jacobean and Caroline manner.

Even in *The Fancies*, however, where plot is so important, it
is noteworthy that there is still too little complication in the
main plot and that there are too many cross-relationships in the
subplots as if to make up for the deficiency.

The lowest of these subplots in a scale of value is that concerning Secco the foolish barber, his associate Spadone, his page
Nitido and his wife Morosa. Ford is repeating himself here.
Nearly all his subplots rely on natural stupidity for part of their
effect and Secco has none of the pathos that makes Bergetto
memorable. The marriage of the young man to the old hag has
also been treated before, and this time it is duller than ever.

Once again it is clear that the subplots have the aim of
stating in a lower key the theme of the main story. Secco's suspicions of the 'honesty' of his wife Morosa, like Romanello's
misinterpretation of Flavia's conduct in the other subplot, are
obviously connected in some way with the misconstructions of
character which lend such unity as it has to the main Castamela
–Livio–Octavio story. One might even describe the whole play
as a set of variations on the theme of misinterpretation. But the
characters of the main story gain nothing from the contrast—if
it is a contrast—and the whole effect is dissipated.

I cannot share fully Miss Sargeaunt's admiration for the
Flavia story. Undoubtedly Flavia's parting from her former
husband Fabricio, of her continued affection for whom she has
given no public sign, is one of the most memorable moments in
Ford. As Fabricio leaves—and it is Flavia who has suggested
that he should go—she turns to her second husband Julio:

| | |
|---|---|
| *Flavia* | Prithee *sweetest* |
| | Harke in your eare—beshrew't, the brim of your hat |
| | Strucke in mine eye—*Dissemble honest teares* |
| | *The griefes my heart does labour in*—smarts |
| | Vnmeasurably. |
| *Julio* | A chance, a chance, 'twill off; |
| | Suddenly off, forbeare, this handkercher |
| | But makes it worse. |
| *Camillo* | Wincke madam with that eye, |
| | The paine will quickly passe. |
| *Vespuci* | Immediatly, |
| | I know it by experience. |
| *Flavia* | Yes, I find it. |

                                                   (III. 1268–80)

Nor would I deny Ford's success in bringing out the pathos of
her situation. She has been disowned by a bankrupt husband
who has sworn in Court a precontract to another, in order to
justify a separation from his wife, since he believes that she will
not bear poverty with him. Her own feelings have never been
consulted:

> Did I complaine?
> My sleeps between thine arms, were even as sound,
> My dreames as harmelesse, my contents as free,
> As when the best of plenty crown'd our bride bed.
> Amongst some of a meane, but quiet fortune,
> Distrust of what *they call their owne*, or Iealousie
> Of those whom in *their bosomes* they possesse
> VVithout controule, begets a selfe unworthinesse;
> For which feare, or what is worst desire,
> Or paultry gaine, they practise art, and labor to
> *Pander their own wives*: those wives whose innocence
> Stranger to language, spoke obedience onely,
> And such a wife was *Flavia* to *Fabritio*.
>                                   (II. 590–602)[4]

So she makes the best of her second marriage, to Julio, because
Julio loves her.

But her brief comment when she hears that Fabricio has
turned monk

> Hee's now dead to the world
> And lives to heaven, a Saints reward reward him
>                              (V. 2590–1)

[4] Actually Bang's numbering of the lines is wrong here. The series 580–679 is
repeated. But I have thought it better to let the error stand.

is not as successful in suggesting silent griefs as Ford's quiet comments usually are; it implies rather inadequacy of feeling. And
Ford does not leave the character at that. He makes her affect
a 'ridiculous lightnesse' (IV. 1986), an 'antique carriage' (II.
625), which she explains as necessary to defeat the 'lascivious
Villanies' (IV. 1985) of Camillo and Vespuci. We do not believe
it, and we wonder if she and her brother Romanello really
believe it either, since they forgive Camillo and Vespuci so
easily:

> *Cam.*  My follies are acknowledg'd; y'are a Lady
> Who have outdone example: when I trespasse
> In ought but duty, and respects of service,
> May hopes of ioyes forsake me.
> *Ves.*  To like pennance
> I joyne a constant votarie.
> *Rom.*  Peace then
> Is ratified.
>
> (IV. 2002–9)

Ford has relied on a surprise revelation for its own sake, and
character suffers in the process.

The same criticism may be made of the Castamela story,
although Castamela is a more fully drawn character, in fact one
of the most interesting in Ford. She seems to be imagined as a
girl who combines with youth and complete inexperience of the
world a maturity of feeling beside which most of the men in the
play seem child-like.

So she awakens sympathy when she is first introduced, in the
scene in which she declines the hand of Romanello, and Ford
suggests very well the mental reservations she must be making as
she hears her brother Livio expound, with an unprecedented
lightness of heart, his plans for introducing her to feminine
society:

> *Liv.*  Next *Castamela*,
> To thee (my owne lov'd Sister) let me say
> I have not beene so bountifull, in shewing
> To Fame, the treasure, which this age hath open'd,
> As thy true value merits.
> *Cast.*  You are merry.
> *Liv.*  My jealousie of thy fresh blooming yeeres,
> Prompted a feare of husbanding too charily
> Thy growth to such perfection, as no flattery

|     | Of art can perish now. |
| --- | --- |
| *Cast.* | Here's talke in riddles. |
|     | Brother, th'exposition? |
| *Liv.* | I'le no longer |
|     | Chamber thy freedome, we have beene already |
|     | Thrifty enough in our lowe fortunes, henceforth |
|     | Command thy liberty, with that thy pleasures. |
| *Rom.* | Is't come to this? |
| *Cast.* | Y'are wondrous full of curtesie. |
| *Liv.* | Ladies of birth and quality are suitors |
|     | For being knowne t'ee, I have promised, sister, |
|     | They shall partake your company. |
| *Cast.* | What Ladyes, |
|     | Where, when, how, who? |
| *Liv.* | A day, a weeke, a month |
|     | Sported amongst such beauties, is a gaine |
|     | On time, th'are young, wise, noble, faire, and chast. |
| *Cast.* | Chast? |
| *Liv.* | *Castamella* chast, I would not hazard |
|     | My hopes, my joyes of thee, on dangerous triall. |
|     | Yet if (as it may chance) a neat cloath'd merriment |
|     | Passe without blush in tatling to the words, |
|     | Fall not too broad, 'tis but a pastime smil'd at |
|     | Amongst your selves in counsaile, but beware |
|     | Of being over-heard. |
| *Cast.* | This is pretty. |
| *Rom.* | I doubt I know not what, yet must be silent. |

(I. 484–519)

She holds attention also in her dignified refusal to dance at the shameful marriage of Secco and Morosa; in her anger when she discovers that she has been tricked by Livio into becoming one of the elderly Octavio's bevy of beauty, 'the Fancies'; and in her indignant reception of Octavio:

| *Oct.* | The proffer of a noble courtesie |
| --- | --- |
|     | Is checkt it seemes. |
| *Cast.* | A courtesie? a bondage; |
|     | You are a great man vicious, much more vicious, |
|     | Because you hold a seeming league with charity |
|     | Of pestilent nature, keeping hospitality |
|     | For sensualists in your owne Sepulchre, |
|     | Even by your life time: yet are dead already. |

(III. 1593–1600)

The beginning of Act IV, too, has character interest when Livio, who has been told that Octavio is impotent, begins to

fear that he has been misled and ends up by urging Castamela
to return to the home from which he himself has moved her.
Later in the same act, positions are again the opposite of what
he has expected: he generously offers the hand of Castamela to
Romanello, whom previously he has discouraged—only to be
refused.

But there are too many inversions. And the final twists of
plot—when Octavio reveals that the Fancies are really his
nieces, and Castamela and Octavio's nephew, Troylo, confess
their love and apologize for their 'secrecie'—have nothing at all
to do with character. Even Castamela has become a puppet and
surprise is all.

Indeed, one suspects that in *The Fancies* Ford is not above
deliberate deception of the audience. Such deception is the only
apparent reason for the concluding conversation of the scene
in which Romanello in disguise appears to the Fancies:

> *Silvia.*           The Gentleman
> Hath been a little pleasant.
> *Clarella.*    Somewhat bitter
> Against our sex.
> *Castamella.* For which I promise him
> A nere proves choise of mine.
> *Romanello.*  Not I your choice.
> *Troylo.*     So she protested Signior.
> *Romanello.*  Indeed.
>
>                                    (III. 1482–90)

An audience will probably take that as dramatic irony, as a
promise that Castamela will in fact marry Romanello, whom
she does not here recognize in disguise. The surprise then when
she does not marry him will be the greater. (It is only on re-
reading that one could hope to see in it some suggestion of an
understanding between Castamela and Troylo even at this
stage.)

*The Fancies*, then, suggests comparison with *The Queen* rather
than Ford's other plays. In spite of success with single characters
and in single scenes, these are the only two which can be
omitted from an edition of his works without any loss whatever
to his reputation. And his last play shows him finally rejecting
this popular kind of drama in favour of one which would at least
allow him room to write as he pleased.

*The Ladies Triall* was almost certainly written early in 1638.
The title-page tells us that it was 'Acted By both their Majesties
Servants'—i.e. The King and Queen's Young Company or
Beeston's Boys—who are first heard of in 1637 and to whom the
play was licensed on 3 May 1638.[5]

We need not take too seriously the description of it in the
Dedication as '*this Issue* of some lesse serious houres'. Ford always
liked to present his dramatic work as a mere secondary interest;
and most of the weaknesses of *The Ladies Triall* are not of the
kind attributable mainly to lack of seriousness but are similar to
those found in his earlier plays. One such weakness is again the
extended use of comic subplots; Act II, for example, is almost all
wasted on them. They are not entirely bad. Ford would not be
Ford if there were not some pathos and knowledge of life in
them, as for example when Martino protests that his 'niece'
(strictly his great-niece) Levidolche[6] is a wanton who is ruining
his name as well as hers, but nevertheless gives in to her tears
against his better reason. Even some of the dignified grief of
*The Lovers Melancholy* echoes in his later words to her:

> Ah thou: but what? I know not how to call thee,
> Faine would *I* smother griefe, and out it must,
> My heart is broke, thou hast for many a day
> Been at a losse, and now art lost for ever:
> Lost, lost, without recovery.
>
> (v. 2290-4)

These subplots, then, are in themselves better than some others
in Ford, and they are notably nearly all in verse, as if he wished
to raise their tone; but they are still superfluous, even when one
sees that Malfato's justified suspicion that Levidolche is not
virtuous is set against Auria's unjustified suspicions of Spinella,
and Levidolche's selfish urging of Benatzi to take vengeance on
Adurni and Malfato set against Aurelio's disinterested incite-
ment of Auria to revenge himself on the same Adurni. There is
not even this excuse of contrast for the further plot of the lisping
Amoretta and her suitors.

The main story alone holds our interest. Auria, 'a noble
Genoese' and elderly, leaves his newly-wedded young wife

[5]Bentley, i. 324-5.
[6]Sometimes called Lenidolche in the text.

Spinella and goes off to the wars. He claims that there is financial necessity for his departure:

> My wants doe drive me hence
> (I. 247),

and he swears that this is why he must go:

> By that sacred thing
> Last issu'd from the Temple where it dwelt,
> I mean our friendship, I am sunke so low
> In my estate, that bids me live in *Genoa*
> But six moneths longer, I survive the remnant
> Of all my store.
> (I. 258–63)

But he is not given the last word on this subject, and Aurelio,
who, like Fernando in *Loves Sacrifice*, has been hailed as 'a friend,
a perfect one' (I. 235–6) but better deserves the title, takes a
very different view.

*Aurel.* For that so, but you have a wife, a young,
A faire wife; she, though she could never claime
Right in prosperitie, was never tempted
By triall of extreames, to youth and beauty,
Bayts for dishonour, and a perisht fame.

*Auri.* Shew me the man that lives, and to my face
Dares speake, scarce thinke, such tyranny against
*Spinellas* constancie, except *Aurelio*
He is my friend.

*Aurel.* There lives not then a friend
Dares love you like *Aurelio*, that *Aurelio*,
Who late and early; often sayd and truly,
Your marriage with *Spinella* would entangle
As much th'opinion due to your discretion,
As your estate, it hath done so to both.

*Auri.* I finde it hath.

*Aurel.* He who prescribes no law,
No limits of condition to the objects
Of his affection; but will meerly wed
A face because tis round, or limb'd by nature
In purest red and white, or at the best,
For that his mistresse owes an excellence
Of qualities, knowes when and how to speake,
Where to keepe silence, with fit reasons why,
Whose vertues are her onely dowre, else
In either kinde, ought of himselfe to master
Such fortunes as adde fuell to their loves

           For otherwise:—but herein I am idle,
           Have foold to little purpose.
*Auri.*   She's my wife.
*Aurel.*  And being so, it is not manly done
           To leave her to the triall of her wits,
           Her modestie, her innocence, her vowes.
           This is the way that poynts her out an art
           Of wanton life.
*Auri.*   Sir, sayd yee?
*Aurel.*  You forme reasons,
           Iust ones, for your abandoning the stormes
           Which threaten your owne ruine; but propose
           No shelter for her honour; what my tongue
           Hath utterd, *Auria*, is but honest doubt,
           And you are wise enough in the construction.
*Auri.*   Necessitie must arme my confidence.

                                        (I. 279–321)

No doubt the sentiments of Futelli and Piero about the folly
of risking 'a bloudy nose of honour' (I. 107) have the effect of
swinging sympathy to Auria, whose attitude contrasts so well
with theirs. But although we admire his courage and know that
a worthy wife will remain constant in absence, there is from the
beginning this suggestion that Auria is partly to blame for what
follows; and he himself accepts Aurelio's advice to the extent of
giving Spinella a full caution about her behaviour during his
absence lest it be misinterpreted. Miss Cochnower[7] is not justified in regarding Auria as an ideal character (he certainly falls
far below the ideal later).

When Auria is away, Adurni makes love to Spinella while he
is entertaining her. She rejects his advances, not, like Biancha,
in terms that suggest an unwilling admiration but scornfully
and with finality:

           *Auria, Auria,*
           Fight not for name abroad, but come my husband,
           Fight for thy wife at home.

                                        (II. 1056–8)

Aurelio finds them together and, his mind having been running
along these lines from the start, jumps to the wrong conclusion.
Spinella rejects a suggestion from Adurni that he should act as
her champion:

                    [7]Op. cit., pp. 132, 157, 188.

*Ad.*    Lady, be not mov'd,
      I will stand Champion for your honour, hazard
      All what is deerest to me.
*Spin.*          Mercie heaven!
      Champion for me, and *Auria* living? *Auria?*
      He lives, and for my guard my innocence
      As free as are my husbands clearest thoughts,
      Shall keep off vaine constructions.

                                     (II. 1116–23)

(The parallel with *The Queen* will be as obvious as is the improvement.)

There is to be no bloodshed; and indeed here, at the end of Act II, the action of the play is nearly over—because Ford's interest is not in action but once again in the psychological problem to which the action has given rise.

Spinella vanishes and pity is skilfully aroused for Auria, who can say that he has risked his life to be able to afford comforts for her and has won them, but now sees that it would have been better for them to stay together, even at the cost of poverty:

           Would she and *I* my wife,
      I meane, but what alas talke I of wife,
      The woman, would we had together fed
      On any out-cast parings, course and mouldy,
      Not liv'd divided thus, I could have beg'd
      For both, for't had been pitty she should ever
      Have felt so much extremitie.

                                     (III. 1414–20)

In a splendid scene which is given up entirely to the tracing of Auria's emotions, he begins by defending Adurni and Spinella against Aurelio's charges. Then he blames Aurelio for interfering, then assumes that they are guilty and loses his self-control.

      For *I* am certaine, certaine it had beene
      Impossible, had you stood wisely silent,
      but my *Spinella,* trembling on her knee,
      Would have accusd her breach of truth, have beg'd
      A speedy execution on her trespasse,
      Then with a justice lawfull as the magistrates,
      Might I have drawne my sword against *Adurni,*
      Which now is sheathed and rusted in the scabberd;
      Good thankes to your cheape providence, once more
      I make demand———my wife———you——sir.

                                   (III. 1509–18)

But when Aurelio stands firm:

> What I have done, was well done and well meant;
> Twenty times over, were it new to doe.
> Ide doo't and doo't, and boast the paines religious;
> Yet since you shake me off, I slightly value
> Other severity
>
> (III. 1526–30)

Auria's rage collapses.

Auria is again the centre of interest in an equally good later scene when Adurni comes before him and Aurelio to confess his own guilt and plead Spinella's innocence.

> *Adur.*  My errand hither is not
> In whining trewant-like submission,
> To cry I have offended, pray forgive me,
> I will doe so no more: but to proclaime
> The power of vertue, whose commanding soveraignty,
> Sets bounds to rebell bloods, and checke restraines,
> Custome of folly by example teaches
> A rule to reformation; by rewards,
> Crownes worthy actions, and invites to honour.
> *Aure.*  Honour and worthy actions, best beseeme
> Their lips who practice both, and not discourse 'em.
> *Auri.*  Peace, peace, man, I am silent.
>
> (IV. 2128–39)

Perhaps the most important lines in the play occur as Adurni reaches his conclusion:

> *Auri.*  Who can you thinke I am? did you expect
> So great a tamenesse as you finde, *Adurni*,
> That you cast lowd defiance? say—
> *Adur.*           I have rob'd you
> Of rigor (*Auria*) by my strict self-penance,
> For the presumption.
> *Auri.*           Sure Italians hardly
> Admit dispute in questions of this nature,
> The tricke is new.
>
> (IV. 2185–93)

The trick *is* new. One might almost say that it is Ford's particular contribution to Jacobean drama. Auria is a Hamlet without even Hamlet's sudden bursts of energy. In *Loves Sacrifice* Ford had worked within the limits of the Elizabethan tragedy of blood; but here, at the end of his career in *The Ladies Triall*, the wife really is innocent, the friend is disinterested and the

husband has some judgment; and it becomes apparent that, in
spite of the occasional violence of action in his earlier plays,
Ford never was interested in the tragedy of blood. He was not
interested in murders; in fact he was not particularly interested
in what people do. His concern was with what they think and
feel. But to make a play only from what people think and feel
is to strain drama to its utmost limits. As Professor Ellis-Fermor
has suggested, Ford had reached the very frontiers of drama.

Spinella is restored to Auria (of whose grief she has been
told). At first he insults her, but they reason it out and all ends
happily, although for some reason best known to Ford, Adurni
is married to Spinella's sister Castanna. Auria says that he
wishes this marriage so that there can be no suspicion that he is
jealous of Adurni. Perhaps things do happen that way in real
life, perhaps Ford no longer cared; the play for him was over
once Auria and Spinella had come together again. It is difficult
enough to accept as plausible Spinella's forgiveness of Aurelio:

> **Aure.**          You will pardon
>       A rash and over-busie curiositie.
> **Spi.**    It was too blame, but the successe remits it.
>                                  (v. 2542–4)

It is impossible to believe in the falser reconciliation in the subplots, and the play collapses.

We need not therefore, with Schelling, class *The Ladies
Triall* as a comedy while Ford's other plays are regarded as
tragedies or decadent romances. Its ending is, one might say,
simply irrelevant. Nor is it necessary, with Parrott and Ball, to
class *The Ladies Triall* and *The Fancies Chast and Noble* as 'social
comedies' to be explained by 'his friendly rivalry with Shirley
and his admiration for Jonson' (p. 248). These two plays are
just as serious as and no more comic than his others; they represent only further extensions of the methods he had always used,
with perhaps the difference that whereas in *Loves Sacrifice*, for
example, he had accepted a whole conventional set of actions,
in *The Ladies Triall* he writes to please himself until the end and
only then succumbs.

No doubt, as Miss Sargeaunt has said, the main plot of *The
Ladies Triall* is also 'too slight' (p. 76). More important than the
fact of slightness, however, is the reason for it. Ford could easily

enough have lengthened his plot with surprises, in the manner of *The Fancies*. He wisely chose not to repeat that mistake. Unfortunately, however, he still filled out the play with subplots, the reintroduction of which from time to time one here comes to dread, so absorbing is the main story. In this again he was simply bound by tradition; he wrongly believed, with Bird, the writer of his prologue, that

> Language and matter, with a fit of mirth,
> That sharply savours more of aire than earth,
> Like Midwives, bring a Play to timely birth.

Once the continual surprises of *The Fancies* had been ruled out as a suitable way of constructing a play, the alternative to this mixing of plot and subplot was the creation of an entirely new kind of psychological drama and the finding of a new kind of 'action' into which to translate it, with its own shape, its own climax, its own continuity. If we remember how even with the experience of centuries behind him, a dramatist like Eugene O'Neill has still been unable fully to solve that problem (witness a play like *Strange Interlude*), we shall be less inclined to criticize Ford for his 'failure'.

# X

## FORD'S ACHIEVEMENT

THERE is perhaps no better way of beginning to appreciate Ford's contribution to the drama of his day than by comparing his work with that of the playwrights who were his true contemporaries, Philip Massinger and James Shirley. Little as we know of Ford himself, it is clear that his whole approach to dramatic composition was different from theirs. He may be seen as a gifted amateur, a genius or near-genius who wrote plays in his spare time, partly no doubt because he needed the money but mainly because he felt an over-powering need for self-expression in some form of literary art. Massinger and Shirley were professional dramatists. Both, being university men, were at least as well educated as Ford but they knew actual want and wrote prolifically for a living. Both, too, were closely connected with the theatre itself. Shirley was still a pathetic figure in theatrical circles after the Restoration; after the death of Fletcher, Massinger became chief playwright for the King's Men for some thirteen years. As a result, Shirley in his three dozen plays and Massinger in his two dozen acquired a professional competence—'slickness' might even be the better word—that Ford never attained.

Competence was, perhaps, more easily acquired in the kind of play that Massinger and Shirley favoured. I do not wish to seem to underrate a comedy like *A New Way to Pay Old Debts*, nor would I willingly pass over Shirley's achievement in comedy, where in plays like *The Witty Fair One*, *Hyde Park* and *The Lady of Pleasure* he showed the way to Etherege and Congreve; but I think it will be agreed that the typical Caroline drama was rather a play like Massinger's *The Renegado*. The briefest summary of this will show how different it is from Ford.

The action takes place in Tunis—exotic settings being, of course, highly favoured in tragi-comedy. In Act I, a Venetian, Vitelli, learns of the arrival in Tunis of Grimaldi, the Renegade, who has previously sold Paulina, Vitelli's sister, to the Viceroy. When the Sultan's niece, Donusa, shows an interest in him,

Vitelli encourages her, in the hope that this will enable him to release Paulina. Act II tells of Vitelli's willing surrender to the seductive Donusa, and also of the fall from favour of Grimaldi, who quarrels with the Viceroy. In Act III, Donusa and the already penitent Vitelli are betrayed and imprisoned; and in Act IV, Donusa, having at her trial demanded the right to save her life by converting Vitelli to her religion, is herself converted by him to Christianity. Then, in the final Act, Paulina pretends to the Viceroy that she will turn Turk and in return asks that the execution of Vitelli and Donusa be postponed for twelve hours and Donusa be committed to her care. She sends to the imprisoned Vitelli a packthread baked in a pie; with the thread, let down from the apparently quite unguarded window, he draws up a rope; and they all escape in the vessel which the penitent Renegade has seized, the Turkish crew being duly stowed under hatches. (One might almost be reading a novel by Rafael Sabatini.)

It is obvious that this is a tissue of improbabilities: there happen to be none of those sudden revelations of identity so common in Massinger but in addition to the various conversions and the unlikely escape, we have to believe that the Turkish Viceroy refrains from violating Paulina, because he is convinced that the holy relic she wears round her neck will protect her. It will also be obvious that in such a play subtlety of characterization will find no place. Our interest is held only by the mere sequence of events in time; and it is typical of Massinger's and his audience's entire absorption in 'what happens next' that it should take four consecutive scenes in Act II to get Vitelli in to Donusa in her palace, although already in Act I she had told him how it would all be managed. In Act II, scene i, her servants agree to help her; in the second scene, Vitelli passes through the two sets of guards by using Donusa's name as password; in the third, the servants receive him; and in the fourth, he and Donusa actually meet.

This, then, is a splendid example of the kind of play on which Ford finally turned his back in *The Ladies Triall*. I think it will be clear how far his methods differed from those of Massinger's well-made tragedies and tragi-comedies in which each act had its own highlight and plots were arranged for the sake of sur-

prise, even if entirely new motives had to be introduced as late
as the fifth act. Nor was Ford interested in 'such killing stories'
(to use Shirley's own phrase) as that of *The Traitor* where nearly
all the characters are murdered so that no guilty person is left in
power at the end. It is also noticeable that he avoids the typical
Caroline plots where attention is concentrated on mere in-
triguers like Lorenzo or the Cardinal or Francisco; in these, it is
almost impossible to create the sense of tragic waste. He had, in
short, seen the fallacy in the theory which Shirley was to advocate in his prologue to *The Cardinal*:

> A poet's art is to lead on your thought
> Through subtle paths and workings of a plot.

Had Ford been writing *The Cardinal*, he would certainly have
made more of the problem of the Duchess Rosaura, whose un-
desired suitor, Colombo, is probably a better man than the one
she loves; had he been writing *The Duke of Milan*, Francisco's
wish to kill Sforza would not have been almost casually
explained at the last minute as the desire to take vengeance on
the man who had seduced his sister. The plays would, in short,
however less satisfactory in other ways, have had far greater
intellectual and emotional depth.

Ford's achievement was that within the limits of the dramatic
tradition of his time and without even relying extensively on
soliloquy, he went so far towards a pure concentration on states
of mind. To describe that concentration merely as a taking of
the drama indoors, into halls and bedchambers, and to see it
as a mere 'effeminizing' of drama, is to be guilty of misrepresen-
tation;[1] and yet that error, it might almost be said, has been the
root of all that is wrong in Ford criticism. 'Each of the tragedies
and tragi-comedies of Beaumont and Fletcher', Professor L. C.
Knights has said, 'is a series of cunningly contrived situations
to exploit, not to explore and express emotions; and that is
decadence'.[2] Ford may not be the equal of Beaumont and
Fletcher in cunning contrivance of situation; but that is at least
in part because his gift *is* the exploration, rather than the ex-
ploitation, of human passion.

There are, of course, limits to Ford's interests even within the

[1] Sherman, Bang, *Materialien*, xxiii. p. viii.
[2] *Drama and Society in the Age of Jonson* (London, 1937), p. 295.

field of what we now call psychology. He has not the quick eye
of Shirley and Massinger for social differences; nor indeed,
although *Perkin Warbeck* touches on the subject, does he seem
to have been curious to inquire into the causes of social good
and evil. But it cannot be a handicap to a dramatist that he is
interested in people as individuals, even if he is not attracted by
all of them.

One is tempted to say of Ford, as Mr F. L. Lucas has said of
Webster, that his passion was for 'passion itself'; but the phrase
is unfortunate as used of either dramatist if it seems to imply an
interest only in violent emotions or emotions violently expressed.
The passion of which Ford most frequently writes—of which
Jacobean and Caroline dramatists most frequently write—is
tragical love; but we should remember also the grief of Huntley,
the regret of Ithocles for his youthful impetuosity, the quiet
scorn of Castamela for her brother's easily-induced change of
mood, and the scenes in which Warbeck, Biancha and Calantha,
particularly, meet death.[3] Ford's range of emotion is not really
as narrow as some might pretend. It is noticeable, in fact, that
if he has a preference, it is for those at the end of the emotional
scale that is opposite to violence; he consciously chooses again
and again as his principal characters men and women whose
emotions are not of the obvious kind and who are at first glance
not likely to provide good dramatic material. For his success
with them he deserves all the more credit. His women, particularly, are probably second only to Shakespeare's; they are
certainly far above those Massinger heroines of whom Arthur
Symons so rightly said (in his introduction to the 'Mermaid'
selection) that they are always talking about their virtue as if it
were something 'detached and portable'—as if virtue were 'a
sort of conscious and painful restraint' (pp. xxii, xxvii).

It has been suggested (for example, by Professor Hardin
Craig in *The Enchanted Glass*, New York, 1936) that Ford's
psychology is limited by his belief in the then widely-held
Stoical doctrine of the passions, according to which 'one passion
of the heart replaced another as one liquid might replace

[3]Stoicism in facing death is one subject that appeals to most Elizabethan
dramatists, from Kyd onwards; it is a favourite theme, of course, with Webster and
Tourneur, whose handling of it provides the closest parallels to Ford's.

another in the emptying and filling of a cup.'[4] No doubt instances from his plays could be quoted in support of this view, but one wonders whether the explanation is not too simple; and '*Tis Pitty*, however exceptional it may be, does prove that Ford when he chose could trace convincingly the development of emotion over a period of time. But this is not typical; and what I believe is true of his work in general is that he was concerned to portray not the sequence of emotions but the single, static feeling—in revealing which, Middleton of the later dramatists was possibly his only rival. Continuity, then, was not Ford's strength or interest. Massinger may sincerely have believed that a man would always be converted if you aimed at him a long enough diatribe; but the conversions and repentances in Ford, I feel, are the result not of psychological inadequacy so much as of dramatic casualness.

It was surely natural that a man who had this special interest and who had already shown, in the plays he had written in collaboration, that his skill lay in dissecting the emotion of a character under stress, should have constructed as his first unaided drama a play like *The Lovers Melancholy*. This (and I believe the same is true of *The Broken Heart*) gave him a series of climaxes, as it were, a number of independent scenes of the kind in which he knew that he could excel. From each is drawn its full emotional content and the impression is not, as in a Massinger tragi-comedy, of rapid progression from one day to the next. But Ford saw that the price he was paying was a certain artificiality; the plays give the sense of conscious manipulation, of not moving, as it were, of their own momentum. Accordingly, he experimented along lines that led to '*Tis Pitty*, the one play, I would maintain, in which he achieved the dramatic straight line. It is as if Ford had worked back from something like the 'pattern' of tragi-comedy in *The Lovers Melancholy* and, even, *The Broken Heart* to the kind of continuous plot that gave the sense of inevitability to great Elizabethan tragedy. I do not suggest that he necessarily saw it in this way; what is almost certain is that he found his perfect dramatic model in *Romeo and Juliet*. Yet having found it, he continued to experiment: in *Perkin Warbeck* the onus of the plot is, as it were,

[4]Quoted from the English edition (Blackwell, Oxford, 1950), p. 116.

transferred to history; and in *The Ladies Triall*, he hardly worried about plot at all. Almost as in a play by Bernard Shaw, dialogue here is action, the only action. Without a greater inventiveness than Ford possessed, there was simply not enough to sustain a full five-act drama; without the subplots the play would have been impossible.

Ford may be seen, then, as a constant experimenter with dramatic form, who, because he never quite cast off the shackles of Elizabethan and Jacobean drama, did not find the new form he was seeking. His dissatisfaction is, however, clearly shown not only by his final play or even by his differences from his contemporaries but also by the way in which, in nearly all his plays, he tries to relate the subplots to his main story; by stating in them, in a minor key, the theme of his play, he does make what could, if followed up, have been an important contribution to later drama.

It is significant that the technique has, in fact, become popular—in the modern novel; and the novel might, as many have suggested, have provided Ford with the scope that drama, in a way, denied him. Had he written novels, however, they would have been of a special kind. The novel to which the dramatic art of Massinger approximates is the simple story of adventure; Ford anticipated rather the slow-moving analysis of a Richardson. But he is a far more sophisticated artist than Richardson: perhaps his delicate presentation of Penthea in *The Broken Heart* could more fitly be compared with Virginia Woolf's drawing of Mrs Ramsay in *To the Lighthouse*.

Yet it would be very wrongheaded to wish that Ford had written novels rather than plays. For, in addition to his well-nigh incomparable gifts for exposition of character through dialogue, drama gave him scope for his poetry; and his best poetry is produced when he writes for the stage. The improvement from the non-dramatic work to *The Lovers Melancholy* is particularly significant here. Thereafter he does not change very much; poetically, perhaps, he never surpassed *The Lovers Melancholy* and *The Broken Heart*.

Of Ford's dramatic verse one cannot say, as one can say of the verse of Massinger and Shirley, that it too marks a decline from the standards of the great Elizabethans, that it is half-way

towards prose. Ford's verse is pitched higher than the verse of
his contemporaries; and although he uses the extra syllable very
frequently, he does not, like Massinger, make a practice of
ending lines with an unaccented tenth syllable (e.g. a preposi-
tion). The five-stress pattern of the blank verse line is always
clear.

His particular gift is a quite exceptional clarity and simplicity,
even—or particularly—in moments of the greatest emotional
stress. If the well-known speeches of Penthea, Calantha or
Warbeck be analysed, it will, I think, be found that they are
also most economical in their imagery. Ford uses extensive
imagery only when characters are speaking, as it were, artifi-
cially, as when Thamasta makes her approaches to Eroclea:

> The constant Loadstone, and the Steele are found
> In seuerall Mines: yet is there such a league
> Betweene these *Minerals*, as if one Veine
> Of earth had nourisht both. The gentle Mirtle
> Is not ingraft vpon an Oliues stocke:
> Yet nature hath betweene them lockt a secret
> Of Sympathy, that being planted neere,
> They will both in their branches, and their rootes
> Imbrace each other; twines of Iuie round
> The well growne Oake; the Vine doth court the Elme;
> Yet these are different Plants. *Parthenophill*,
> Consider this aright, then these sleight creatures,
> Will fortifie the reasons I should frame
> For that vngrounded (as thou think'st) affection,
> Which is submitted to a strangers pitie.
> True loue may blush, when shame repents too late,
> But in all actions, Nature yeelds to Fate.
>
> (*The Lovers Melancholy* III. 1385–1401)

The difference between this and Thamasta's normal speech is
that between Macbeth's when he is playing a part and
Macbeth's when he is not.

When Ford's characters speak from the heart, with no need
to camouflage or conceal their feelings, they always do so with
a remarkable directness. There is a scarcity of imagery, even
of adjectives; and a high proportion of the words become, as in
the great poetry of Vaughan, monosyllabic. This can be illus-
trated from any of the speeches quoted before as examples of
Ford's tragic power, such as

> I thanke thee too, *Eroclea*, that thou would'st
> In pitie of my age, take so much paines
> To liue, till I might once more looke vpon thee,
> Before I broke my heart
> (The Lovers Melancholy, v. 2572-5)

and it is no different in the violent *Loves Sacrifice*:

> I am beholding to you, that vouchsaf'd
> Me, from a simple Gentlewomans place,
> The honour of your bed: 'tis true, you did;
> But why? 'twas but because you thought I had
> A sparke of beauty more then you had seene.
> To answer this, my reason is the like,
> The selfe same appetite which led you on
> To marry me, led me to loue your friend.
> (v. 2455-62)

This same simplicity of expression to convey the deepest feelings is also seen to be the secret of Calantha's famous death-speech (a secret known perfectly well, of course, to Shakespeare, Webster and Tourneur):

> When one newes straight came hudling on another,
> Of death, and death, and death, still I danc'd forward,
> But it strooke home, and here, and in an instant . . .
> They are the silent griefes which cut the hart-strings;
> Let me dye smiling.
> (The Broken Heart, v. 2588-90, 2594-5)

Simplicity is one of the qualities that make such passages perfectly adapted for speaking on the stage: a great actor could achieve much with them, although the rhythm and the wording alone are quite able to suggest the emotion.

Of tragic poetry at this level not many even of the Elizabethan, Jacobean and Caroline dramatists were capable. And it is debatable whether Ford fails more than once or twice to write poetry of this order when the situation calls for it. That is why no play by him, however carelessly it may be constructed or however unsuitable it may be for him as a whole, is ever unprofitable reading. His poetry alone would, then, earn him his place in English literary history. What study of his dramatic career reveals, however, is not satisfaction with his ability to write great verse but a never-ended search for the kind of play in which this tragic poetry might most fitly and most fully obtain expression.

The closest parallel before the twentieth century is to be found, I think, not in the work of any Jacobean or Caroline dramatist but in Robert Browning's attempts to fit within the limits of the stage play his characteristic expositions of character in verse; and, significantly, Browning's search led him away from the theatre to the set piece like *In A Balcony* and ended really in a return to the dramatic monologue (or, perhaps, series of monologues, in *The Ring and the Book*). *In A Balcony* is particularly interesting here because, in its analysis of the tragic effects on the Queen of a wrongly induced belief that Norbert loves her, it shows precisely the kind of subtlety in the presentation of feminine character that we expect from Ford; and Browning can achieve this only by abandoning all pretence at writing for the theatre, by limiting his characters to three, and by allowing all three of them long self-expositions of as many as thirty-five lines at a time.

Ford, in the days when drama was paramount, took the opposite way out; and there is no reason for believing that any of *his* plays failed on the stage. He did successfully compromise with the requirements of the theatre. Taking full advantage of the opportunities which drama offered him, he almost overcame its limitations.

The last word might well be left with Swinburne (p. 405):

No poet is less forgetable than Ford; none fastens (as it were) the fangs of his genius and his will more deeply in your memory. You cannot shake hands with him and pass by; you cannot fall in with him and out again at pleasure; if he touch you once he takes you, and what he takes he keeps hold of; his work becomes part of your thought and parcel of your spiritual furniture for ever; he signs himself upon you as with a seal of deliberate and decisive power.

# APPENDIX

## The Duke of Lerma

*The Great Favourite, or, The Duke of Lerma*, a play by Sir Robert Howard which was produced and published in 1668, formed no part of Ford studies until Professor Alfred Harbage published his 'Elizabethan—Restoration Palimpsest' in *The Modern Language Review*, xxxv, July 1940, 287–319. 'As it is,' Harbage wrote, 'I feel sure that admirers of John Ford have another play to read' (p. 304).

The general argument of the article is that many Elizabethan (including Jacobean and Caroline) plays, both in print and in manuscript, were available to Restoration dramatists in search of material to adapt. Such adaptations were frequent but were only rarely acknowledged and then not always adequately. Many Elizabethan manuscripts are known to have been in the hands of publishers; and once one of these found its way to a playwright, any borrowing from it could not be traced. Harbage suggests that *The Duke of Lerma* is an example of such rewriting.

The play has long been known, but perhaps mainly because its preface forms part of the literary debate between Howard and Dryden on the subject of rhyme in drama. (An interest in this debate has, for example, led to the modern edition of the play, by D. D. Arundell, in his *Dryden and Howard 1664-1668*, Cambridge, 1929.) Harbage argues that it is also worth study as a rewriting by Howard of a play by Ford.

It is certain that *The Duke of Lerma* is not entirely Howard's work. Howard confesses as much in his prefatory note 'To the Reader'.

For the *Subject*, I came accidentally to write upon it; for a Gentleman brought a *Play* to the *King's Company*, call'd, *The Duke of LERMA*; and by them I was desired to peruse it, and return my Opinion, whether I thought it fit for the *Stage*: After I had read it, I acquainted them, that in my Judgment it would not be of much Use for such a Design, since the Contrivance scarce would merit the Name of a *Plot*; and some of that, assisted by a Disguise; and it ended abruptly: and on the Person of *Philip* the *III*ᵈ there was fix'd such a mean Character, and on the Daughter of the Duke of *Lerma*, such a vitious one, that I cou'd not but judge it unfit to be presented by any that had a Respect, not only to Princes, but indeed to either Man or Woman; and about that time, being to go into the Country, I was perswaded by Mr. *Hart* to make it my Diversion there, that so great a Hint might not be lost, as the Duke of *Lerma* saving himself in his last Extremity, by his unexpected Disguise, which is as well in the true Story as the old *Play*; and besides that and the *Names*, my altering the most part of the *Characters*, and the whole *Design*, made me uncapable to use much more; though perhaps written with higher Stile and Thoughts, than I cou'd attain to.

Moreover Dryden has some relevant comments on it in *A Defence of an Essay on Dramatic Poesy* (not all of which Harbage quotes):

As for the play of *The Duke of Lerma*, having so much altered and beautified it, as he has done, it can justly belong to none but him. Indeed, they must be extreme ignorant as well as envious, who would rob him of that honour; for you see him putting in his claim to it, even in the first two lines:

> Repulse upon repulse, like waves thrown back,
> That slide to hang upon obdurate rocks.

After this, let detraction do its worst; for if this be not his, it deserves to be. For my part, I declare for distributive justice; and from this and what follows, he certainly deserves *those advantages which he acknowledges to have received from the opinion of sober men.*

In the next place, I must beg leave to observe his great address in courting the reader to his party. For intending to assault all poets, both ancient and modern, he discovers not his whole design at once, but seems only to aim at me, and attacks me on my weakest side, my defence of verse.

To begin with me,—he gives me the compellation of *The Author of a Dramatic Essay*, which is a little discourse in dialogue, for the most part borrowed from the observations of others: therefore, that I may not be wanting to him in civility, I return his compliment by calling him *The Author of the Duke of Lerma.*

(Everyman's Library, p. 61)

Dryden is clearly sneering at Howard and denying his authorship of the play as a whole; and *The Duke of Lerma* is far better than any other Howard has written, even if it is very typical of minor Restoration drama in one or two of its love scenes in rhyme, such as II. ii.

It may also be suspected that Howard is in part spoiling an original. There is some mislineation of the blank verse which, splendid at times, halts at others. And perhaps the device of the

Duke's use of the Cardinal's robes to save his life had more point in the old play than in Howard's.

There is not much doubt that the old play from which Howard said he began was Elizabethan (in the widest sense). Although Howard was fond of blank verse and says that he wrote *The Duke of Lerma* partly in it, partly in couplets, he would hardly have written this kind of verse. Moreover the Duke is obviously yet another Elizabethan malcontent of the villain-hero kind. (Arundell is surely wrong, in view of Lerma's attempted prostitution of his daughter, in calling him 'the honest great man, who is forced to aim at villainy by the devotion of his servant, and who can still command respect even at the end'–p. 208).

The historical events dealt with in the play go up to at least 1624. Harbage would say 1629 because 'a hint in the last scene indicates that the playwright was aware that Maria Calderon bore Philip a son'. But this does not seem to follow merely from the King's words to Maria in v. ii:

> *Spain's* empty Throne,
> Unless from you, shall want succession.

This is simply part of his proposal to Maria, who is in any case only a dramatist's rough equivalent for the actual mistress of Philip, who was an actress and not the daughter of the Duke of Lerma. Hence the range of time from which we may select an author of the original play is not quite as narrow as Harbage would have us believe.

Indeed, I question many of the probabilities which seem to him to suggest that Ford wrote the original.

The first of these is the purely negative evidence. Only Massinger, James Shirley or Ford, Harbage claims, would have won such praise from Howard—i.e. of those writing after 1629. But once remove that limit and the field is far wider. Nor am I quite convinced by Harbage's elimination of Shirley on the grounds that if the original had been his 'we would probably have had its licensing record, and it would probably have been published (as was *The Politician*, in 1655). Shirley was co-operating with Moseley in the issuing of his plays' (p. 299, note 5). I shall return to the question of Shirley.

Secondly, there is the argument that the theme of *The Duke of Lerma*—exposing chastity to danger—is a favourite with Ford and is most like *The Fancies Chast and Noble*. Harbage surely strains probability, however, in comparing Lerma's escape from justice by his becoming Cardinal with the incident in the sub-plot of *'Tis Pitty* in which the Cardinal saves Grimaldi from justice after the murder of Bergetto. A better parallel, I am sure, would have been Maria's defiance of Medina when he threatens to murder her, wrongly believing her unchaste, and Biancha's defiance of the Duke in *Loves Sacrifice*. No doubt, too, Ford would have been interested in the situation of a father urging his daughter to become a King's mistress in order to save her father's life. But, after all, chastity in danger is one of the great Elizabethan subjects; and one can see just as many parallels, for example, between *The Duke of Lerma* and the scene in Shirley's *The Traitor* in which Sciarrha pretends to urge his sister Amidea to become the mistress of the Duke that she may save her brother's life (II. i.).

Thirdly, the characterization is said to be like Ford, and Philip is compared to Palador, pining for love. But the two have not much in common, and the whole question is complicated by the fact that in *The Duke of Lerma* there is some historical basis for the characters, however altered they may be. And if it be suggested (as Sensabaugh has suggested[1]) that there is some influence of Burton on the characterization, then the answer might be again that it is easy to show that Shirley, too, was well acquainted with Burton's work. I may also refer to the evidence of *Andromana* that still other playwrights were using Burton for dramatic purposes just before the Civil War.

Finally, Harbage finds many parallels to Ford in the style. Particularly, he points out that Ford's distinguishing manner-ism of 'd'ee' occurs in *The Duke of Lerma* at least three times (II. i., IV. i., v. ii.)—and it may be significant that it is altered to 'd'ye' in the 1692 edition.

Again, 'A Traitor to my trust' from *The Duke of Lerma* is com-pared to Ford's typical construction 'traitor to honour', 'traitor to friendship' and so on. But to use this mannerism to help to distinguish Ford's work from another's in a known collaborate play is one thing; to use it to suggest Ford here is another. For in

[1] 'Another Play by John Ford', *Modern Language Quarterly*, iii (1942), 595–601.

Shirley's *The Traitor* again I find 'A treason to our friendship'
(I. i.) and almost on successive pages of *The Royal Master* 'a rebel
twice to virtue' and 'is there no friend to goodness?' (v. ii.).

Far more convincing are the lines of Medina, in IV. i.:

> Tis pitty forces me to this Violence,
> The pitty of thy Blood, I had a share in
> Before it was infected with this Leprosie.

Harbage is, of course, able to quote many lines from Ford in
which lust is thus described as leprosy. Even here, however, one
must remember, with Miss Sargeaunt, that 'such an idea as
leprosy as a stain to be washed off with tears, which occurs
often in Ford's plays, has its origin deep in the roots of biblical
and liturgical thought and expression' (p. 47). And it is easy to
put alongside Medina's:

> thy heart
> So very foul, that it needs pious washing
> (*Duke of Lerma*, IV. i.)

Shirley's lines:

> my hands shall mutiny,
> And boldly with a poniard teach my heart
> To weep out a repentance
> (*The Traitor*, II. i.).

I have made a close study of *The Duke of Lerma* in an attempt
to clinch the case for Ford but can only conclude that it must
stop far short even of probability. To Harbage's list of similarities, one could add perhaps the masque of Medina (presented
in the hope of bringing Maria to see the error of her supposedly
sinful life with the King); possibly the use of Shakespearian
reminiscence:

> And I will gladly tell you my true Story,
> Like those that with a pleasure do repeat
> The Tales of mighty Dangers they have past
> (IV. i.);

a few phrases such as

> Come, *Maria*, my Best, my Dear *Maria*
> (II. i.)

—compare

> Come mine owne best *Fernando*, my deere friend
> (*Loves Sacrifice*, III. 1806)—

and one or two images. For example,

> There is some Mole,
> That heaves for us unseen
> (III. ii.)

*may* recall, from *The Lovers Melancholy*,

> Ye worke and worke like Moles, blind in the paths,
> That are bor'd through the crannies of the earth . . .
> (II. 1058–9);

and imagery using deer, lions, the viper and cobwebs could all be paralleled from Ford. Lerma in IV. ii. refers to the 'fawning Rascals' of the Court

> which like Cobwebs
> Shou'd be swept off;

King Henry in *Perkin Warbeck* (v. 2129) mentions 'Cobweb Parasites'. But these are largely conventional, and the Mole image, for one, appears elsewhere in Howard:

> Heaving like labouring moles within the Earth
> (*The Surprisal*, III. iv.)

Indeed, it may be suspected that as many similarities as this could be found between *The Duke of Lerma* and the plays of many other good Jacobean dramatists. I would submit the following in addition to those already given, from one play by James Shirley.

(1)   He that seeks Safety in a States-man's pity,
 May as well run a Ship upon sharp Rocks,
 And hope a Harbour
> (*Duke of Lerma*, v. ii.)

Pity the seaman, that to avoid a shelf
Must strike upon a rock to save himself
> (*The Traitor*, IV. ii.).

(2)    here are the parts of my full Ruine,
 These decay'd Out-Houses shew the chief Building
 Wants Reparation
> (*Duke of Lerma*, I. i.)

my soul is but one flame
Extended to all parts of this frail building
> (*The Traitor*, II. i.)

(3) Medina says Maria's conduct will

> disturb
> The ashes of her sleeping Mother
> (*Duke of Lerma*, II. ii.)

> But all the ashes of
> My ancestors do swell in their dark urns,
> At this report of Amidea's shame
> > (*The Traitor*, II. i.)

(4)   From henceforth, Sir, be every body's King,
       And then you are your self
       > (*Duke of Lerma* III. ii.)

> Oh, take yourself again, Sir; use your greatness
> To make the hearts of Florence bow to you
> > (*The Traitor*, III. iii.).

The imagery, which I had hoped would settle the question—even with Howard intervening—proved in fact most disappointing (in both senses—much of the imagery of *The Duke of Lerma* is used mechanically). It is necessary to say also that there are many metaphors and similes which are unlike both Ford and Howard; and I venture to think that if one were forced to nominate the author of such a grim rejoinder as

> *Alcara*   These fainting fits seem as if she were
>              With Child.
> *D'Alva*   With Death I fear
> > (II. ii.)

one would nominate both Webster and Tourneur before Ford. And Webster was writing at least until 1625; Tourneur died early in 1626.

The further limitation to all this inconclusive discussion based on internal evidence is the simple fact that we have a reference to a play on the subject of the Duke of Lerma that could have been available to Howard. But it is not said to be by Ford. It is *The spănish Duke of Lerma* which (together with '*The Duke of Guize, The Dumb Bawde* & *Giraldo y*ᵉ *Constant Lover*') was entered by Moseley on the Stationers' Register, on 9 September 1653, as by Henry Shirley. The play is significantly missing from Warburton's later list.

To the obvious question why it could not have been this play by Henry Shirley that Howard was rewriting, Harbage offers two answers. One is that Henry Shirley, who was murdered in 1627, could not have written the original of Howard's *Duke of Lerma* which refers to events in 1629. I have already shown that this dating is not so certain, and after all Howard could have added the one phrase from which so much is inferred, particu-

larly as he says the old play ended too abruptly. The second
answer is that Henry Shirley was not a good enough dramatist.
This somewhat hasty generalization is based on his one surviving play, *The Martyr'd Souldier*, which is certainly well below
the level of *The Duke of Lerma* as it now stands and—except
possibly for one or two similes and a similar deliberate echoing
of Shakespeare

> Wee'le live together if it please the King,
> And tell sad Stories of thy wretched Mother
> (Act III, sig. E4)—

bears no stylistic resemblance at all to the Howard play. But it
is referred to as an old play (in the address 'To the Reader of
this Play now come in Print') and spoken of in terms that suggest
that it goes back a long way.[2] It could, then, have been an
early attempt by Henry Shirley, whereas *The Duke of Lerma*, if
his, obviously came at the close of his career. (Incidentally,
another of the plays given him by Moseley, *The Dumb Bawde*,
was almost certainly *The Dumbe Baud of Venice* which was played
at Court by the King's Men on 15 April 1628[3] and it was for the
King's Men that a play called *The Duke of Lerma or y'e spanish
Duke* was protected by the Lord Chamberlain on 7 August 1641.[4]
Of course Ford was writing for the King's Men in 1628, too.)

At any rate, Harbage argues that Moseley was wrong in his
ascription of the play to Henry Shirley. It is, however, very
difficult to see why he should deliberately ascribe to so minor a
playwright a work by a major one. Alternatively, if the ascrip-
tion was merely a slip, then it is much easier to imagine that
Henry Shirley was a mistake for James Shirley than for John
Ford; and the entry immediately before *The spanish Duke of
Lerma* in Moseley's list is in fact *The Polititian* by James Shirley.
I think I have shown that *The Duke of Lerma* has as many
parallels to James Shirley as to Ford; I know no Elizabethan,
Jacobean or Caroline drama which has as many similarities to
*The Duke of Lerma* as has *The Traitor*.

If Ford wrote *The spanish Duke of Lerma* by himself, as Harbage
suggests, between 1630 and 1634, then he apparently did not

[2] I am aware that the same address is found appended to another play printed
by the same printer in 1637.
[3] Bentley, i. 96, 130.
[4] Bentley, i. 66, 130.

think highly enough of it to publish it—and the parallel would be *The Queen*. If, on the other hand, he was concerned with the play, in its way a topical drama like *A Late Murther*, shortly after 1624, then it was almost certainly in collaboration. And all the strong parallels with Ford's other plays in *The Duke of Lerma* do cluster in a few scenes: II. i., IV. i., IV. ii. and V. ii.— three of these including the tell-tale 'd'ee', and the four of them amounting to much the same proportion of a total play as we have seen Ford contributing in his other collaborate work. One cannot finally rule out the hypothesis that *The spănish Duke of Lerma* was written by Henry Shirley and John Ford in collaboration—which would justify Moseley's entry. Nor is it completely impossible that, if the rewriting were three or four years before publication, Sir Robert Howard had the assistance of James Shirley (particularly if James Shirley were related to Henry— which seems probable, although it is not likely that James was Henry's son, as Fleay conjectured). The parallels with James Shirley are more widely distributed through *The Duke of Lerma*; and his 'knowledge of the profession was . . . taken advantage of by dramatic amateurs, such as the Duke of Newcastle and the Hon. Edward Howard, though to what extent we cannot now discover.'[5]

But these conjectures are rash. I am concerned mainly to enter a caveat against too ready an acceptance of Professor Harbage's ascription of the original play. We must agree with him, however, that *The Duke of Lerma* is well worth reading and be grateful that he has brought it to the notice of lovers of Ford.

[5]Gosse, Introduction to *James Shirley* in the 'Mermaid' series (London, 1888), p. xxvii.

# INDEX